# COMMUNICATING CHRIST IN SIMPLICITY

PETER UNOARUMHI

# COMMUNICATING CHRIST IN SIMPLICITY

# COMMUNICATING CHRIST IN SIMPLICITY



**Printed in Nigeria**



ISBN. : 979-8-40851-619-3



Book layout designed by:
Grace Springs Africa Publishers
P.O. Box 696, Shomolu, Lagos, Nigeria.

Tel: 09090567143, 08141381091
info@gracespringsafricapublishers.com
www.gracespringsafricapublishers.com

# DEDICATION

To my wife and pillar of support, **Becky Unoarumhi,** for partnering with me by making the home front harmonious while allowing me the freedom to manage my writing, and to spread the Good News of Jesus Christ in an enabling environment. You are truly irreplaceable.

To all those who have a desire to glorify and share the truth of Jesus Christ passionately!

# ACKNOWLEDGEMENTS

A heartfelt thank you to Jesus Christ, the Author and Finisher of our faith, for enabling the writing of this book.

To friends of Jesus Christ: My pastors and their wives, leaders of Cornerstone Anointed Church of Christ, and to the entire Cornerstone family, whose encouragement, prayers and support have made this book a reality. I say a big thank you.

I deeply appreciate the editorial team: Becky Unoarumhi, John Chijioke Ijioma, and Olumide Savage, whose input and relentless effort made this book a success.

My gratitude also goes to my children, Manuela, Debra and Joshua. I love you all!

# CONTENTS

CHAPTER ONE

# THE CHURCH'S GREATEST NEED TODAY

The church evangelism team clasped their hands together as they gathered in a huddle. With their heads bowed and their eyes closed, the leader of the group offered a prayer to God to crown their planned door-to-door witnessing with success. With that done, they dispersed in groups of two into different sections of the neighbourhood. It was a monthly ritual, and one the church leadership harped on as part of its church growth strategy.

At a corner on one of the streets, two of the "street evangelists" met a lady (probably in her late 20s or early 30s), and for the next 20 to 30 minutes, gave her a biblical exposition from Genesis to Revelation on why she needed to accept Jesus Christ as her Saviour and Lord.

The young lady listened patiently to them and even seemed to nod in agreement at some points during the preaching. Typically, they concluded their message with an invitation for her to accept Jesus Christ into her life, hoping to register her decision and quickly move on to the next person. She smiled politely at them but declined the invitation. She was not interested, or better still, she was not just ready to make that decision yet. They pressed her for a response but she still would not budge. She politely excused herself, leaving the two evangelists frustrated and confused.

A similar scenario was playing out as two members of the evangelism team were frantically labouring to persuade an elderly man to repent of his sins and avoid the judgment of hellfire. "All sinners will go to hell," they reminded him. The man was unfazed; in fact, he did not dispute their message. "I know," the man calmly admitted. According to him, "That is where my ancestors are, and I am preparing to join them there."

Devastated, the witnessing duo had nothing more to say and had no choice but to leave the man alone. The last of the evangelism team also met a brick wall witnessing to a middle-aged, working-class couple. In their sermon, the witnessing duo had told the couple what miracles of blessing and prosperity awaited them in a life in Christ. The man who responded on behalf of the couple was not persuaded. He pointed out to the preachers that he knew several people in the city where he lived who were very wealthy but were not Christians. He told them flat out that he did not have to become a Christian to become rich.

The believers in the above true-life stories are certainly not unique in their struggle to communicate Christ accurately. Almost every Christian who takes the Great Commission seriously has at one time or the other suffered rejection and experienced failure in his/her bid to win people over to Christ. All over the world, the body of Christ wrestles with Jesus' command to preach the gospel to every creature. That command is becoming even more challenging with the rise of secular humanism, terrorism, and growing resentment of Christianity worldwide.

## THE COMMUNICATION PROBLEM

Communication is a major challenge Christians face in evangelizing in this contemporary world. Communication also appears to be at the heart of most human problems and crises. At home, offices, in relationships, in churches, in non-governmental organizations, in government and on the streets, the one major problem the world is facing is communication; either the lack of it or the failure to communicate accurately.

In a survey of divorced couples in the United States, 77% were because of poor communication or a lack of it. Management expert, Peter Drucker says, "70% of all management crises are the result of poor or inadequate communication." In her book, Clearly Communicating Christ, Landa Cope observes that "many of the most deeply rooted problems we have, chronic conflicts in the world, revolve around communication issues, between groups, between male and female, and between God and His creatures." (Page 44)

## WHAT IS COMMUNICATION?

*Webster's New World Dictionary* defines communication as "the act of transmitting" or more specifically "a giving or exchanging of information, signals, or messages by talk, gestures, writing etc." Communication can be verbal as in speaking or preaching, and it can also be non-verbal as in facial expressions such as a smile. In the modern era, it is a combination of the audio-visual forms. It is written in newspapers, magazines, articles, emails, memos, reports, official or personal correspondences. It also can be viewed on your personal computer, on the internet, on the television or it can be heard on the radio. Most authorities agree that communication takes place when the message has been transmitted and the person at the receiving end grasps the intended message.

## IS THE CHURCH COMMUNICATING?

Before His ascension to heaven, Jesus Christ mandated the church to proclaim the message and purpose of His life, death, and resurrection to the world.

> *"Therefore go and make disciples of all nations, baptizing them in the name of the Father and of the Son and of the Holy Spirit, and teaching them to obey everything I have commanded you.*

*And surely I am with you always, to the very end of the age." (Matthew 28:19-20)*

The Lord Jesus gave this commission to His disciples after His resurrection and prior to His ascension to heaven. The command is to "Preach the gospel". The verb "preach" means to herald the message. It is the same word found in 2 Timothy 4:2:

*"Preach the Word; be prepared in season and out of season; correct, rebuke and encourage – with great patience and careful instruction."*

In ancient times, a town crier communicated important messages. This was the king's personal messenger who would cry out the king's message as the people in the town would assemble together, eager to hear the latest information or announcements. The town crier would not give his own message and he would certainly not give his own views or opinions. He would simply give the king's message, word-for-word. He would not interpret the message. It made no difference whether he liked the message or not. His job was to deliver it. He did not debate with people. He did not argue with people. He just presented the king's message. Apostle Paul said:

*"Yet when I preach the gospel, I cannot boast, for I am compelled to preach. Woe to me if I do not preach the gospel! If I preach voluntarily, I have a reward; if not voluntarily, I am simply discharging the trust committed to me. What*

> *then is my reward? Just this: that in preaching the gospel I may offer it free of charge, and so not make use of my rights in preaching it." (1 Corinthians 9:16-18)*

The Message of the gospel drives on the wheel of communication. If we fail to clearly communicate Christ, we have failed in our sacred mandate. With the proliferation of the information instruments and media gadgets, we are making the mistake of thinking that the 21st-century church has excelled in communicating the gospel message. It is true that we have Christian radio and television stations and programmes more than ever before. The church has grown in visibility, numbers, and financial prosperity. We have more conferences, seminars, and programmes that the early church could only imagine in their wildest dreams. With the digital and social revolution, churches and Christian ministries are now able to broadcast the gospel message using such media as the Internet, and devices like iPad, digital satellite television, smartphones and other similar platforms. However, there is a big difference between mass communication and effective communication.

> *"When anyone hears the message about the kingdom and does not understand it, the evil one comes and snatches away what was sown in his heart. This is the seed sown along the path." (Matthew 13:19)*

As the Scripture above points out, communication is deemed to have taken place when the message has been received and understood by the audience. Sending the message is only half the battle; it must be received and understood. Talking or hearing words is not communication. Being on television or radio can give us the impression that great communication is going on, but if your message is wrong, these media will only help you to amplify or advertise your error.

Over 2,000 years after Christ's ascension to glory, billions of people have still not been reached with the gospel message. For many of them, it is not that they have not heard about Jesus Christ; it is just that they cannot make meaning out of the plethora of voices they are hearing. Why is that so? "Often," remarks Cope "It is not that we have been understood and disagreed with, but we have not been understood at all." (pg. 75). According to Mario Murillo, "the world lies well, and we tell the truth badly." Charles Colson made the point that much of the world's ability to understand their need for God stems from "Christians failure to accurately present Christ's message of the Kingdom of God." And many Christians are unable to accurately present the gospel message because they do not really fully understand the gospel. Hence, the church today is in dire need of skilled communicators to spread the message of Jesus Christ.

> *"So is my word that goes out from my mouth: It will not return to me empty, but will accomplish*

> *what I desire and achieve the purpose for which I sent it." (Isaiah 55:11)*

God's greatest desire is to be known and understood by mankind. And His purpose is for us to come to a loving, intimate relationship with Him. Hence, every effort at preaching the gospel must seek to convey this in such a manner as to reveal His true nature, character, and power. God so much longs to reveal Himself to us that He took the unusual step of stepping aside from His throne in Heaven and clothed Himself with the human body with all of its frailties. God longs for us to know Him in a personal and intimate manner.

> *"Jesus answered: "Don't you know me, Philip, even after I have been among you such a long time? Anyone who has seen me has seen the Father. How can you say, 'Show us the Father'?" (John 14:9)*

> *"This is what the Lord says: "Let not the wise man boast of his wisdom or the strong man boast of his strength or the rich man boast of his riches, but let him who boasts boast about this: that he understands and knows me, that I am the Lord, who exercises kindness, justice and righteousness on earth, for in these I delight," declares the Lord." (Jeremiah 9:23-24)*

Apostle Paul's strong desire and prayer was for Christ to be revealed in us.

*"And you also were included in Christ when you heard the word of truth, the gospel of your salvation. Having believed, you were marked in him with a seal, the promised Holy Spirit, who is a deposit guaranteeing our inheritance until the redemption of those who are God's possession – to the praise of his glory. For this reason, ever since I heard about your faith in the Lord Jesus and your love for all the saints, I have not stopped giving thanks for you, remembering you in my prayers. I keep asking that the God of our Lord Jesus Christ, the glorious Father, may give you the Spirit of wisdom and revelation, so that you may know him better." (Ephesian 1:13-17)*

*"I want to know Christ and the power of his resurrection and the fellowship of sharing in his sufferings, becoming like him in his death." (Philippians 3:10)*

## CHAPTER TWO

# WHAT IS THE GOSPEL?

The word "gospel" means "good news" when translated literally. And the good news is Jesus Christ: The God incarnate who paid the ultimate price to free us from the shackles of sin and dominion of Satan. To understand this properly, it is important we go back to the book of beginnings – Genesis. In this story of creation, we learn that man was created in the image of God.

> *"Then God said, "Let us make man in our image, in our likeness, and let them rule over the fish of the sea and the birds of the air, over the livestock, over all the earth, and over all the creatures that move along the ground." So God created man in his own image, in the image of God he created him; male and female he created them." (Genesis 1:26-27)*

In the Garden of Eden, Adam and Eve enjoyed unhindered access to fellowship with God. The best way to describe it is that they lived right in the presence of

God every day. It was normal for God to come down in the cool of the evening to have fellowship with them. It was life as God had designed it; one of the absolute bliss, peace, and harmony. However, the beauty and tranquillity of the garden were truncated when Satan, man's mortal enemy, sneaked into the garden.

> *"And the Lord God commanded the man, "You are free to eat from any tree in the garden; but you must not eat from the tree of the knowledge of good and evil, for when you eat of it you will surely die."* (Genesis 2:16-17)

Unfortunately, Adam and Eve disobeyed God and ate of the tree of the knowledge of good and evil. Instead of obeying God, they bought into the devil's lie that God was being unfair in not allowing them to eat of the tree of the knowledge of good and evil. It is like that today. Many people reject the idea of sin because they think it is an attempt to deprive them of fun and merriment.

> *"When the woman saw that the fruit of the tree was good for food and pleasing to the eye, and also desirable for gaining wisdom, she took some and ate it. She also gave some to her husband, who was with her, and he ate it. Then the eyes of both of them were opened, and they realized that they were naked; so they sewed fig leaves together and made coverings for themselves. Then the man and his wife heard the sound of the Lord God as he was walking in the garden in the*

> *cool of the day, and they hid from the Lord God among the trees of the garden."* (Genesis 3:6-8)

The entrance of sin into the garden brought catastrophic results. First, Adam and Eve lost the glory of the Lord that had covered them. And we see their feeble effort to replace it with man-made covering from fig leaves. What a tragedy! It is akin to what people do today. They try to work out their righteousness instead of accepting God's free gift of righteousness.

> *"All of us have become like one who is unclean, and all our righteous acts are like filthy rags; we all shrivel up like a leaf, and like the wind our sins sweep us away."* (Isaiah 64:6)

Sin also brought fear into the earth. Before sin came, there was nothing like fear. Adam and Eve lived a life of dominion and boundless joy, but the moment they broke God's commandment the evil presence of fear took over. They had not only lost their place of dominion, but they also had a terrifying fear of the Lord's Presence. Unlike before when they ran to God, Adam and Eve now ran away from God. They were separated from God spiritually. But by far the worst thing that sin brought was spiritual separation from God. God had told Adam:

> *"But you must not eat from the tree of the knowledge of good and evil, for when you eat of it you will surely die."* (Genesis 2:17)

But physically speaking, Adam did not die after he ate of the fruit of the tree of the knowledge of good and evil. In fact, Adam lived to be 930 years old. So obviously, God was not referring to physical death. He was talking about spiritual death. You have to understand that man is a "triune being." He is a spirit; he has a soul, and he lives in a body. Your body is just a container of the real you, which is invisible to the physical eye. It is with your spirit that you contact God. Your soul or mind is the seat of your emotions, will, and intellect, while your body is your earthly suit. It is what enables you to live on this earth.

So what happened at the fall? The moment Adam and Eve sinned, they became separated from God spiritually. In other words, they became spiritually dead. There are three types of death recorded in the Bible. The first is spiritual death, which is separation from God. The second is physical death, that is when a man stops breathing and is committed to mother earth. The Bible says, "Man is destined to die once." (Hebrews 9:27). The third and final death, which the Bible calls the second death or eternal death, is when the spirit of a man is cast into the lake of fire after the Great White Throne Judgment.

> *"But the cowardly, the unbelieving, the vile, the murderers, the sexually immoral, those who practise magic arts, the idolaters and all liars – their place will be in the fiery lake of burning sulfur. This is the second death." (Revelation 21:8)*

*"Blessed and holy are those who have part in the first resurrection. The second death has no power over them, but they will be priests of God and of Christ and will reign with him for a thousand years." (Revelation 20:6)*

*"Then I saw a great white throne and him who was seated on it. Earth and sky fled from his presence, and there was no place for them. And I saw the dead, great and small, standing before the throne, and books were opened. Another book was opened, which is the book of life. The dead were judged according to what they had done as recorded in the books. The sea gave up the dead that were in it, and death and Hades gave up the dead that were in them, and each person was judged according to what he had done. Then death and Hades were thrown into the lake of fire. The lake of fire is the second death. If anyone's name was not found written in the book of life, he was thrown into the lake of fire." (Revelation 20:11-15)*

## ADAM'S TRANSGRESSION, HUMANITY'S BURDEN

For us to properly grasp the doctrine of salvation, it is important that we understand sin for what it really is, especially in the light of recent claims by some schools of thought in the behavioural sciences, which claim that man is basically good. They blame the problem of evil and suffering in the society not on man's sinful condition, but on societal pressures, bad parenting, economic inequalities, and prevailing negative sociological conditions in the society. But God who is the creator of man and who is the Sovereign owner of the universe knows better than any social scientist. He declares that human beings, although created pure and noble are all under the power of sin.

> *"Nevertheless, death reigned from the time of Adam to the time of Moses, even over those who did not sin by breaking a command, as did Adam, who was a pattern of the one to come."* (Romans 5:14)

When Adam sinned, his spirit man became dead to God, and he could no longer contact God. This marked the turning point in the history of the human race as man painfully came under the influence and power of Satan, God's archenemy. As a result of Adam's sin, every man that was born into the world inherited Adam's sinful nature. This was what David alluded to when he wrote in Psalm 51:5:

> *"Surely I was sinful at birth, sinful from the time my mother conceived me."*

Each one of us is born sinful and separated from God. That is why we lean naturally to doing wrong rather than right. For instance, you don't teach a child to lie, steal, be jealous, manipulate others or get angry. It just comes naturally to him/her as a result of the congenital disease of sin that was passed down to every one of us from our parents.

*"What shall we conclude then? Are we any better? Not at all! We have already made the charge that Jews and Gentiles alike are all under sin. As it is written: There is no one righteous, not even one; there is no one who understands, no one who seeks God. All have turned away, they have together become worthless; there is no one who does good, not even one." "Their throats are open graves; their tongues practise deceit." "The poison of vipers is on their lips." "Their mouths are full of cursing and bitterness." "Their feet are swift to shed blood; ruin and misery mark their ways, and the way of peace they do not know." "There is no fear of God before their eyes." (Romans 3:9-18)*

The conclusion of the matter is:

*"For all have sinned and fall short of the glory of God." (Romans 3:23)*

The great Apostle Paul catalogued the devastating effects that sin has unleashed on mankind since the fall of Adam in the garden in this manner:

*"They have become filled with every kind of wickedness, evil, greed and depravity. They are full of envy, murder, strife, deceit and malice. They are gossips, slanderers, God-haters, insolent, arrogant and boastful; they invent ways of doing evil; they disobey their parents;*

> *they are senseless, faithless, heartless, ruthless. Although they know God's righteous decree that those who do such things deserve death, they not only continue to do these very things but also approve of those who practise them." (Romans 1:29-32)*

Does that not sound like a description of the world we live in today? In our quest for unrestrained freedom, we willfully violate and despise rules, laws, values and traditions. This has resulted in the strife, malice, bitterness, conflicts, hunger, deprivation, murders, debauchery and depravity that besiege humanity. The breakdown in social order in contemporary society is the terrible consequences of sin in man. As a result, the world is full of broken individuals, broken communities, and broken nations. As one commentator observed:

"People are capable of impressive acts of courage, compassion, and justice. But the ultimate standard against which people must be measured is not human standard, but God's Holy Character, His moral perfection. Good behaviour turns out to be the exception rather than the rule." (Contemporary English Version)

In fact, so soon after the fall, God observed "how great man's wickedness on the earth had become, and that every inclination of the thoughts of his heart was only evil all the time." (Genesis 6:5). What a serious indictment!

## CHRIST TO THE RESCUE

Getting saved - salvation - is one theme that runs throughout the entire Bible. The whole of the Bible is actually the story of man's rebellion and God's plan for redemption and restoration. Soon after Adam's fall, God in His infinite mercy and unfailing love set a plan in motion whereby man could be rescued from the effects of sin and be reconciled to Him.

> *"And I will put enmity between you and the woman, and between your offspring and hers; he will crush your head, and you will strike his heel." (Genesis 3:15)*

This prophecy was referring to God's redemption plan in Jesus Christ. But before Christ came, God had to institute a temporary or stop-gap measure whereby man could receive atonement for his sins and maintain fellowship with Him.

Under the old covenant, He gave the people of Israel a set of rules and regulations that governed their worship, their relationship with Him, and their social relationships with one another. These were summarized in the Ten Commandments. However, the people struggled with sin because of their twisted spiritual condition brought about by the fall of man in the Garden of Eden. To deal with the sin problem, God instituted animal sacrifices to make atonement for their sins. But there was a problem.

> *"The law is only a shadow of the good things that are coming – not the realities themselves. For this reason it can never, by the same sacrifices repeated endlessly year after year, make perfect those who draw near to worship. If it could, would they not have stopped being offered? For the worshipers would have been cleansed once for all, and would no longer have felt guilty for their sins. But those sacrifices are an annual reminder of sins, because it is impossible for the blood of bulls and goats to take away sins." (Hebrews 10:1-4)*

The array of sacrifices was inadequate. It only covered their sins; it did not remit them neither did it remove their sin nature. The animal sacrifices were meant to pacify God; they could not satisfy Him. The blood of bulls and goats could not take away the sins of the people because man was not made in the image of goats and bulls. Man was made in the image of God. Man is not on the same level as animals that were created for his use and benefit. As a result, the yearly sacrifices, apart from not being able to rid them of their sin nature, only added to the people's frustration as they came face to face with their dead spiritual condition in that no matter how hard they tried they could never fulfil the terms of the covenant. Paul captures this dilemma succinctly.

> *"I do not understand what I do. For what I want to do I do not do, but what I hate I do. And if I do what I do not want to do, I agree that the law is*

*good. As it is, it is no longer I myself who do it, but it is sin living in me. I know that nothing good lives in me, that is, in my sinful nature. For I have the desire to do what is good, but I cannot carry it out. For what I do is not the good I want to do; no, the evil I do not want to do – this I keep on doing. Now if I do what I do not want to do, it is no longer I who do it, but it is sin living in me that does it. So I find this law at work: When I want to do good, evil is right there with me." (Romans 7:15-21)*

There was nothing wrong with the law. In fact, according to Romans 7:12, "the law is holy, and the commandment is holy, righteous and good." The problem was with those who were to keep the law. They were imperfect people.

*"But when the time had fully come. God sent His Son, born of a woman, born under the law, to redeem those under the law, that we might receive the full rights of sons." (Galatians 4:4-5)*

*"She will give birth to a son, and you are to give him the name Jesus, because he will save his people from their sins." (Matthew 1:21)*

Jesus Christ came to redeem, or if you like, ransom us from the slave market of sin. He was the Perfect Man who lived a perfect life of obedience and fulfilled all of the law on our behalf (Matthew 5:17). To cap it all, He died on our behalf to take away the penalty of sin.

> *"For the wages of sin is death, but the gift of God is eternal life in Christ Jesus our Lord." (Romans 6:23)*

Under the law, Jesus did not deserve to die because He lived a perfect, sinless life. It was the community of sinful humanity that was under the judgment of God and therefore deserved to die. But since we could not pay the price, Christ did it on our behalf. It is called the Great Exchange.

> *"God made him who had no sin to be sin for us, so that in him we might become the righteousness of God." (2 Corinthians 5:21)*

Jesus Christ was the perfect substitute for our sin. He willingly took upon Himself the form of a man and voluntarily laid down His life to fulfil the just requirements of a righteous and Holy God. Jesus Christ was the Ransom God paid for our sin. I am sure you have heard of kidnappers who demand ransom for their hostages to be released. It was the same with us. We were held captive by Satan in the slave market of sin and the blood of Christ was the ransom that released us from captivity. Why do I say so? The Bible says, "Without the shedding of blood there is no forgiveness." (Hebrews 9:22). That is the reason why the blood of Christ shed on the cross of Calvary has the power to save us.

> *"But with the precious blood of Christ, a lamb without blemish or defect." (1 Peter 1:19)*

The Bible draws a parallel between the Blood Sacrifice of Christ and the sin offering that was offered in the Old Testament, where the Israelites were mandated by God to present animal sacrifices that were perfect without spot or blemish. What that means is that you could not under the Mosaic Law offer an animal that was diseased or defective in any way. In the same manner, Jesus Christ was the only sacrifice acceptable to God because He was untainted with the Adamic stain of sin, having been born of the Virgin Mary through the supernatural operation of the Holy Spirit. The Scripture paints a picture of things the blood of Christ accomplished for us.

> *"For the life of a creature is in the blood, and I have given it to you to make atonement for yourselves on the altar; it is the blood that makes atonement for one's life. Because the life of every creature is its blood. That is why I have said to the Israelites, "You must not eat the blood of any creature, because the life of every creature is its blood; anyone who eats it must be cut off." (Leviticus 17:11, 14)*

> *"How much more, then, will the blood of Christ, who through the eternal Spirit offered himself unblemished to God, cleanse our consciences from acts that lead to death, so that we may serve the living God!" (Hebrews 9:14)*

> *"But if we walk in the light, as he is in the light, we have fellowship with one another, and the*

> *blood of Jesus, his Son, purifies us from all sin." (1 John 1:7)*
>
> *"And from Jesus Christ, who is the faithful witness, the firstborn from the dead, and the ruler of the kings of the earth. To him who loves us and has freed us from our sins by his blood." (Revelation 1:5)*

Now, all we need to do is place our faith in the finished work of Christ on Calvary and accept His offer of grace to give us a new life, free of sin and death. The good news is that God gave each of us a chance to come clean and be at peace with Him when He sent His Son, Jesus Christ, to pay the ultimate price for our sins. There is a heavy price to pay for sin, the price of being dead forever, eternally separated from God. But when we believe in our hearts and confess our faith in Christ, our Spirit is regenerated by the supernatural operation of the Holy Spirit. We become born again.

> *"Therefore, if anyone is in Christ, he is a new creation; the old has gone, the new has come!" (2 Corinthians 5:17)*

A new creation does not mean that if you were short before you became born again, you would now become tall; or if you were dark in complexion you would suddenly become light-complexioned. It simply means that your past has been wiped out; God no longer remembers your sins. As far as He is concerned, they don't exist anymore. You have been made anew through the propitiation of Christ's blood. Once your faith is in Christ, when God looks at you, He sees an entirely new person through the Blood Sacrifice of Christ, and because of Christ you now have right standing with Him. The old habits and character traits that characterize your life in the past are becoming extinct. The Spirit man is recreated through the supernatural operation of the Holy Spirit and the person is alive once again to God. The proof of the new birth experience is readily visible. The born again person suddenly begins to love the Word of God, longs to be in God's presence, enjoys the fellowship of believers, loves to share his new found faith with other people, and generally wants to live a life that is pleasing to God. It is called the miracle of the new birth.

With His sacrifice at the cross, Christ has reversed the curse which came through Adam.

> *"But the gift is not like the trespass. For if the many died by the trespass of the one man, how much more did God's grace and the gift that came by the grace of the one man, Jesus Christ, overflow to the many! Again, the gift of God is not like the result of the one man's sin: The judgment followed one sin and brought condemnation, but the gift followed many trespasses and brought justification. For if, by the trespass of the one man, death reigned through that one man, how much more will those who receive God's abundant provision of grace and of the gift of righteousness*

> *reign in life through the one man, Jesus Christ." (Romans 5:15-17)*

The free gift of righteousness is not like the offence, because it is not transmitted naturally. It involves the active participation of our will. To become saved, all we need to do is acknowledge the substitutionary role of Christ, accept that He died on our behalf and place our faith in His accomplished work on Calvary's cross. Please note that we can never do anything to qualify for the salvation of God.

> *"Not by works, so that no one can boast." (Ephesians 2:9)*

Salvation is not earned; it is received as a free gift from God. It is not by works. Our acts of charity and all our religious activities and obligations should only flow out of our faith in the finished work of Christ, but not to make us righteous before God. The only thing that makes us righteous before God is the Blood of Christ that was shed for the remission of our sins. That should make us glad. Imagine if salvation were by works, some of us would boast of the great things we had to do or go through to qualify for it. The rich will boast of how much they spent or invested to get it. It would make them think they deserve preferential treatment from God. But that is why I like the gospel. It is such a leveller. Whether rich or poor, educated or illiterate, black or white, we are all sinners saved by grace. Hallelujah!

## CHAPTER THREE

# WHAT THE GOSPEL IS NOT

*"He said to them, "Go into all the world and preach the good news to all creation."* *(Mark 16:15)*

Jesus, before His Ascension to Heaven, commanded His disciples to go and preach the gospel to every creature. That command, reported by Saints Mark and Matthew, applies to us today. It is called the Great Commission.

Notice that the command is to "preach the gospel". The word gospel means good news as we have learnt in Chapter 2. To preach means to proclaim the message. As I said in Chapter 2, the town crier was the king's herald or messenger. He walked through the narrow, dust-filled bush paths that qualified as streets in ancient times to shout out the king's message especially in the early hours of the morning.

One important thing to note is that the town crier only delivered the message he was given; he did not give his own opinion, state his desires, or add to the message of the king. Today, it seems as if the church is doing everything except the thing that our Lord told us to do. In many places we have redefined the message, changed it to suit our whims and caprices, altered it to make it more appealing to the people we want to reach. But as someone once said, our job is to make sure that the people get the message; it is not to make them like it. Apostle Paul placed a curse on those who tried to change the gospel message.

> *"But even if we or an angel from heaven should preach a gospel other than the one we preached to you, let him be eternally condemned! As we have already said, so now I say again: If anybody is preaching to you a gospel other than what you accepted, let him be eternally condemned!" (Galatians 1:8-9)*

In our contemporary world, there have been various attempts to give the gospel a total makeover through secular humanisms and other ill-advised man-made methods to make the gospel appealing to people. I will address a few of them in this chapter.

## THE GOSPEL IS NOT ABOUT MEETING SOCIAL NEEDS

Increasingly, more and more ministers and churches are beginning to make the gospel look like it is all about meeting the social needs of the communities where they are located. It has been called the Big Service Movement where churches concern themselves not with preaching the gospel but with feeding the poor, clothing the naked, caring for the sick, providing other social amenities like road and water. There are Christian groups today that are almost exclusively devoted to a social gospel. While we certainly should not be insensitive to the pain, poverty and suffering in the world, yet the social gospel is not what our Lord commanded. The solution to the world's problems is not for each believer to become Mother Teresa.

In an editorial in January 2009, Christianity Today observed that "the greatest social need in the world today is not HIV/AIDS outreach. It is not hunger. It is not global warming, not ending poverty or eliminating malaria or tuberculosis. It is not clean water, racial reconciliation, sexual trafficking or abortion. And it is not peace in the Middle East and not even peace in the world. These are not unimportant social issues. They grab the heart of God. God's compassion has always been focused on the poor and oppressed – something noted all through the Bible. None of these good works or great works deals with the most profound social problem facing mankind. That social problem is **alienation from God**.

"It is, in fact, the first social problem. After Adam and Eve ate of the tree in the midst of the garden, the Lord God with whom they have had warm fellowship seeks them out. But they hide in fear and shame. From this, the Biblical story unfolds to reveal murder, lust, greed, loneliness, pride, oppression, and a host of other evils that plagued mankind. The Biblical picture is clear; the breakdown of society is rooted in the breakdown of our relationship with our creator. And the Biblical response is equally clear: The way out of social chaos begins with being restored to God. For transformed individuals go hand in hand with transforming social networks."

We can feed people, clothe them, give them healthcare, and provide them with shelter, and yet they can still be as lost spiritually as when they were without those things. Besides, there are humanitarian groups and non-governmental organizations that are well known for providing these services. But the church is the only institution that is equipped to preach the gospel.

## THE GOSPEL IS NOT A SOCIAL OR POLITICAL ACTIVISM

There is a growing thought in the church that Christians have been called to change the world. As a result, they should be at the forefront of social and political activism. Hence, they should take charge of the business and economic spheres of society. The idea is that Christians need to exercise dominion in the government and market place to enthrone righteousness in the society and actualize the angelic proclamation in Revelation 11:15 that "the kingdom of the world has become the kingdom of our Lord and of his Christ, and he will reign forever and ever."

It is called Liberation Theology. But is this really our mission? As well-meaning as some of these "Christian activists" may be, what evidence do we have in the Bible for Bible-believing Christians to engage in social protests and political demonstrations to force government and political leaders to adopt Christian principles? There is not one example of the early Christians engaging in political or social activism as a way of influencing the policies of the governments under which they operated. People like Daniel and his three friends as well as the Hebrew midwives engaged in some form of civil disobedience but it was not for the purpose of forcing an ungodly society to obey godly principles.

What does that say of the various Christian groups and alliances that are vigorously campaigning and protesting against abortion, same-sex relationships, child slavery, and official government corruption? What about those whose main preoccupation is to see Christians elected into government? As good and important these things are, they have a tendency to derail us from the main purpose of the church aside from the fact that they have little, if any, lasting results.

> *"The weapons we fight with are not the weapons of the world. On the contrary, they have divine power to demolish strongholds. We demolish arguments and every pretension that sets itself up against the knowledge of God, and we take captive every thought to make it obedient to Christ." (2 Corinthians 10:4-5)*

The early Christians lived under oppressive Roman government and in societies where temple prostitution and all kinds of vices flourished. But what was their main thrust?

> *"Those who had been scattered preached the word wherever they went."* (Acts 8:4)

Apostle Paul said,

> *"Yet when I preach the gospel, I cannot boast, for I am compelled to preach. Woe to me if I do not preach the gospel!"* (1 Corinthians 9:16)

Instead of Christian activism, we need preachers who will preach the uncompromising Word of God to a lost and dying world. We are not to pressure the world to adopt the principles of godliness; we are to win them over to Christ by our message and lifestyle.

Engaging in Christian activism has the potential to present the church as another political lobby group and very often leads to compromise and unholy alliances as some of us may have witnessed recently in the politics of Nigeria. It was said of the early Christians that they turned the world upside down in Acts 17:6. And they did this without engaging in any form of activism whatsoever. The method they used is what we have to adopt today. We are to change the world one person at a time.

> *"Paul entered the synagogue and spoke boldly there for three months, arguing persuasively about the kingdom of God. But some of them became obstinate; they refused to believe and publicly maligned the Way. So Paul left them. He took the disciples with him and had discussions daily in the lecture hall of Tyrannus. This went on for two years, so that all the Jews and Greeks who lived in the province of Asia heard the word of the Lord." (Acts 19:8-10)*

God never told us to change the world. Our mandate is to convert individuals and turn them into Disciples of Christ. They, in turn, will convert other individuals and make them Disciples of Christ. With no finances or political backing but by the power of the Holy Spirit we learn that the gospel spread to the entire Asian region from Tyrannus. We are to preach the gospel "to every creature" (individuals) and when a person responds positively to the gospel message, the Grace of God transforms his/her life.

## THE GOSPEL IS NOT CHURCH GROWTH

Too many people today confuse church growth with evangelism. The former has to do with luring people to be part of a particular church, group or denomination, while the latter presents Christ as the Saviour of the soul. Most of what we have on Christian television could easily pass for a church membership drive. Preacher after preacher engages in desperate, sometimes shameful attempts to lure people to their churches. They use all kinds of gimmicks to project their church as the place to receive healing, miracles and breakthroughs. More, often than not, the focus is the preacher, not Jesus Christ. The preacher is projected as the one that possesses God's supernatural ability to bring healing and deliverance to the unsaved and oppressed; he is hyped as God's channel of blessing to the people.

> *"He said to them, "Go into all the world and preach the good news to all creation." (Mark 16:15)*

Mission and evangelism must be the heartbeat of every local assembly. It should be the lifestyle of every local church and every member of the body of Christ.

Yes, there are those unsaved people who are invited to the church and receive Christ in the process. But we must not see that as justification for not going as commanded or investing in missions and evangelism as we ought to do. In the world, our emphasis should be that of evangelism, but in the church, our emphasis should be primarily that of discipleship. In the world, we should be reaching them. In the church, we should be teaching them. The Saints need to be indoctrinated in the church; the indoctrinated saints need to be evangelizing in the world.

CHAPTER FOUR

# COMMUNICATING CHRIST ACCURATELY

One of the great challenges confronting believers today is communicating the message of Christ in terms that ordinary people can understand. Whether from the pulpit or through televangelism or one-on-one witnessing, it is imperative that we communicate Christ accurately. As we learnt in Chapter 1, often times "it is not that we have been understood and disagreed with, but that we have not been understood at all." At other times, we have muddled up the gospel message and made it say what it does not say. I once read an article in a Christian magazine that perfectly captures the communication crisis in the church today, it reads:

WHICH JESUS DO YOU SERVE?

*By Brendon Powell*

There seems to be more than one Jesus to choose from these days.

Which one is the true Jesus and who am I following?

- There is a **'Seeker Friendly' Jesus.** He is the one who

will not offend anyone in any way; He loves everyone no matter what they do.

- There is a **'Sow and Reap' Jesus.** He made a covenant with man so that man could sow his seed and reap wealth and happiness on earth, and then go to Heaven when he dies.
- There is a **'Blend in with the World' Jesus.** He wants us to look like, act like and be like the world in order to reach the lost.
- There is a **'Never Ending Grace' Jesus.** His 'grace' covers us no matter what we do or how we live.
- There is a **'Just Believe' Jesus.** As long as you truly believe in your heart, you are saved.
- There is a **'Name It, Claim It' Jesus.** You name it; anything and it is yours! If you don't get it, it is because you lack faith, it is your fault.
- There is a **'Carnal' Jesus.** He doesn't expect you to overcome sin; He understands you are just carnal.
- There is a **'Heart Dwelling' Jesus.** All you have to do is ask Him into your heart and right away He's there, you're going to heaven!

I could not agree more with the writer of this article. Various versions of Jesus, different from the true Jesus of the Bible have been presented to an undiscerning public by well-meaning but ignorant people in the name of evangelism. Effective communication of the gospel will always result in an accurate understanding of the person and power of Christ.

## EVANGELISM, OUR PRIMARY CALLING

Communicating Christ accurately is crucial to our God-given mandate to evangelize to the world. A look at what is going on right now shows that we have a lot of inaccurate messages, to the point that some of the souls we thought have been won to Christ are actually not truly born again. What we are experiencing in many places is that churches are gathering crowds but not making disciples. So we have a situation where many of those in churches are there because those churches appear to be the one in vogue or the preacher happens to be a so-called "miracle worker". In a lot of places, many of the presumed converts are following the pastor; there is no real commitment to Christ. How do I know that? I know because many of such people are more committed to the words of the pastor than those of Christ. That is the by-product of faulty communication.

## THE MEANING OF EVANGELISM

The New Testament uses the word "evangelize" in a narrow sense. It defines it as the telling of the good news (the gospel) that Jesus Christ is the Messiah and King. Evangelism is the proclamation of the good news and initiation of people into the kingdom of God through faith and repentance (Luke 4:18, 9:2, 8:1).

> *"The Spirit of the Lord is on me, because he has anointed me to proclaim good news to the poor.*

> *He has sent me to proclaim freedom for the prisoners and recovery of sight for the blind, to release the oppressed."(Luke 4:18)*
>
> *"And he sent them out to preach the kingdom of God and to heal the sick." (Luke 9:2)*
>
> *"After this, Jesus travelled about from one town and village to another, proclaiming the good news of the kingdom of God. The Twelve were with him." (Luke 8:1)*

Evangelism is only a part of the mission. While evangelism is the spreading of the good news, the mission is the outflow of the love of God in word and deed. In essence, to evangelize is to spread the good news that Jesus Christ died for our sins and was raised from the dead as the reigning Lord according to scriptures. He now offers forgiveness of sins and the liberating gift of the Holy Spirit to all who repent and believe.

## THE IMPLEMENTATION OF THE EVANGELICAL MESSAGE

The Bible gives us the Message, the Mandate, the Method and the Means for evangelism.

The Evangelical Message is repentance and forgiveness of sins through the suffering, death and resurrection of Jesus Christ based on the Holy Scripture.

> *"Then he opened their minds so they could understand the Scriptures. He told them, "This is what is written: The Christ will suffer and rise from the dead on the third day, and repentance and forgiveness of sins will be preached in his name." (Luke 24:45-47a)*

The Evangelical Mandate is to share the message with all nations.

> *"To all nations, beginning at Jerusalem."* (Luke 24:47b)

The Evangelical Means is the dynamism of the Holy Spirit.

> *"I am going to send you what my Father has promised; but stay in the city until you have been clothed with power from on high." (Luke 24:49)*

The result when Evangelical Message is implemented:

**Responsible, Reproducing Christian**
**=**
**Responding, Reproducing Congregation**

## THE PURPOSE OF EVANGELISM

The purpose of evangelism is to deliver the lost out of darkness, where Satan enslaves, into God's marvellous light, where Jesus Christ is King.

Therefore, it is also contained in the Scripture,

> *"'See, I lay a stone in Zion, a chosen and precious cornerstone, and the one who trusts in him will never be put to shame.' Now to you who believe, this stone is precious. But to those who do not believe, 'The stone the builders rejected has become the capstone,' and, 'A stone that causes men to stumble and a rock that makes them fall.' They stumble because they disobey the message – which is also what they were destined for. But you are a chosen people, a royal priesthood, a holy nation, a people belonging to God, that you may declare the praises of him who called you out of darkness into his wonderful light. Once you were not a people, but now you are the people of God; once you had not received mercy, but now you have received mercy." (1 Peter 2:6-10)*

It is important that we understand that every born again person has been called into the ministry of evangelism. However, not all Christians are called into the office of an evangelist; it must be by the gift of the Holy Spirit. Something is your gift when the measure of the Holy Spirit deposit is far more than what exists in the average person.

The gospel means good news, so we have been called to communicate the good news of Jesus Christ. God has given one person to everybody and that person is supposed to play the role of the Messiah, the Anointed or the role of the owner of life. That person is Jesus Christ.

Jesus Christ is meant to play the role of "the owner." He owns us, and we do not own ourselves.

God has always been concerned about the people He made. God made man, but man made gods because man refused to be controlled by God. He disobeyed God, thus began the curse of spiritual adultery. Man exercised his imagination to create all manner of gods yet God did not let man go away. He had a plan even from the beginning. Genesis said that there would be a seed from the woman that would bruise the head of the serpent.

> *"And I will put enmity between you and the woman, and between your offspring and hers; he will crush your head, and you will strike his heel." (Genesis 3:15)*

That seed of the woman came in the person of Jesus Christ. When Christ came, He sacrificed His own life for the sin that was committed by man. By His death, He paid for the wages of sin, which is death. Whether then or now, the wages of sin is death, but the good news is that somebody has died for us. If this is not communicated and believed by us, then we do not belong to Christ. If we do not have confidence that we have been saved by the death, resurrection and ascension of Christ, it means that we do not even understand that going to heaven is based on the finished work of Christ. It is because Christ died for our sins that we will be found in heaven. It is not because we have the power to obey any law.

When Christ came as a baby, born through the Virgin Mary, He entered the system of this world through the theory of incarnation, even though He had always been. Now the Word that had always been but was not seen became flesh. The Word became flesh means that somebody that was never seen came to be seen. When He came to be seen, He died for our sins. When He rose by the power of the Spirit, He sent the same Spirit that brought about His resurrection to guide and rule over us. That is the good news. Everybody must know how to tell this story in various ways and to various people, being careful to be accurate.

## THE ACCURACY OF CONTEXTUALIZATION

Any student of history, particularly church history knows that the only faith that existed in the early days of the church was universal faith called Catholicism. The word Catholic means universal. But at some point in the history of the church, paganism and all kinds of idolatry were mixed with the Christian faith. That generated some protest by some who felt the doctrine of Christ had been compromised.

The early church people were portraying Jesus Christ as a messenger of the gospel in Catholicism. But the apostles that saw Him did not present Him like that in the scriptures. The Protestants felt that this was not an accurate representation of the Lord and Saviour, Jesus Christ. In protesting and getting away from Catholicism, we went into the time of reformation and afterwards all kinds of other branches of the protestant movement such as the Anglicans, the Baptist and the Pentecostals emerged.

The gospel is Jesus Christ Himself. He is the good news, not the messenger of the good news. If you believe there is another mediator through whom we can go to God, then it means Jesus was a messenger of the good news. But the good news is Jesus Christ! We know Him, we learn everything about Him and we do all His will because He has saved us. In winning souls, the problems we have been having is instead of presenting Jesus Christ, we present His church. Instead of presenting Jesus Christ, we present what He hates, and what Jesus hates is not the good news.

What we should preach is what Jesus has done for mankind and that refers to the saving work of God in Christ.

> *"For God so loved the world that he gave his one and only Son, that whoever believes in him shall not perish but have eternal life. For God did not send his Son into the world to condemn the world, but to save the world through him. Whoever believes in him is not condemned, but whoever does not believe stands condemned already because he has not believed in the name of God's one and only Son. This is the verdict: Light has come into the world, but men loved*

> *darkness instead of light because their deeds were evil. Everyone who does evil hates the light, and will not come into the light for fear that his deeds will be exposed. But whoever lives by the truth comes into the light, so that it may be seen plainly that what he has done has been done through God." (John 3:16-21)*

If Christ is not well presented or communicated, then we are not preaching the good news. Sadly, there are churches that are more interested in getting more people into their fold rather than presenting Christ accurately. They are interested in getting more people to obey the laws they believe in, than to experience the true freedom we have been given in Christ. They say things like, "If you do not do this then you do not belong to us."

There are people, even among Pentecostals, who instead of presenting Christ, focus on shirts and trousers and other disputable issues. There are people who you can tell are so blind, they do not even know that Christ is all that matters.

It is all for Him, all by Him throughout our lifetime. We have this myriad of issues going on and God is saying to us, 'I want all the people that belong to me to come back to Christ and communicate Him; proclaim Christ and reveal Christ.'

A truly born again Christian is supposed to be able to see how Christ fits into what is before him because Christ is the life of everybody in the world. He is the owner of life and He made life. He died for life and rose to justify life. So in presenting Christ, everybody must know how He fits into the issue or matter before him or her. We are not to present any other thing. That is what evangelism is about!

You need to know how to tell the story well and tell it again and again in various contexts. If somebody is telling the good news and then veers off to bad news such a person is not well schooled and it so often happens.

Here is an example. Somebody presenting Christ may start by quoting 'For God so loved the world that He gave His one and only son, that whosoever believes in HIM shall not perish but have eternal life' (John 3:16). But in the very next second, the person says to the female hearer, "do you think you can go to heaven when you fornicate or do you think you can make heaven with your trousers? Who is deceiving you?" That is presenting bad news in the same context with the good news. Such preachers have forgotten that in the stories we have in the Bible, an armed robber went to paradise with Christ without baptism. Jesus did not go to a party in the house of the righteous; instead, He went to a party in the house of a sinner called Zacchaeus and He took him in as a member of His apostolic team. Why? He came to save the sinner; He did not come to condemn. Anytime the message of condemnation resonates more than the good news, then there is miscommunication.

The gospel is centred on the grace of Jesus and not the condemnation of Satan. Sometimes, because of the anger we may have against sin, we are tempted to condemn, forgetting that we are not the judge. The judge of life is saying, "Go and present the good news because I came for good tidings." Many of us in the church feel condemned sometimes because of what we heard in the past.

Sin has been condemned but a sinner has been justified in Christ. When we present the gospel along this line, we give hope to sinners. That is not to say we condone sin but the emphasis should be on the good news and not the law that breeds fear. The law was not good news because nobody could keep it. The law was introduced to bring man to the end of himself and accept he needed a Saviour, and when Christ fulfilled it and took our place on the cross, God expects that we should appreciate Him.

It is so sad that Christ is not appreciated; He is not being presented and communicated well. All of us must be accurate communicators of Christ; of course, we must first be persuaded before we can communicate this message properly.

## THE BEAUTY OF CHRIST

We are all meant to discharge the role of an evangelist. It is supposed to be easy to tell the story of Jesus Christ who is the life of all. If we are condemning sinners, rather than presenting the quality life of Christ to them, then we are presenting bad news and that means we are not communicating Christ effectively. Nobody will go to a place that is hopeless or not attractive. So, the aim of the good news is to reveal the attractiveness of God in Christ.

If Christ is not attractive, why should people come to Him? All the qualities that Christ claimed as the Messiah were very attractive.

> *"Jesus said to her, "I am the resurrection and the life. He who believes in me will live, even though he dies." (John 11:25)*

This statement is so attractive; it means death cannot hold us captive because He rose from the dead. As a result, we also will rise from death into eternity.

> *"I am the bread of life." (John 6:48)*

This means our lives cannot be sustained by mere bread. But He has given us His life which is eternal and by which bread and drinks is also put on our table. People want to eat and they need to understand that Christ, who is the Head of the church, provides for His people who believe in Him. Make Christ attractive and do not let people run away from Him.

> *"When Jesus spoke again to the people, he said, "I am the light of the world. Whoever follows me will never walk in darkness, but will have the light of life." (John 8:12)*

When we see someone in darkness, our responsibility is to give hope by presenting Christ as the light. Present the result instead of emphasizing the problem. Present the answer; Christ is the answer. Don't just witness or communicate; be accurate and effective. A lot of communication going on right now concerning Christ is faulty. That alone will prevent some people from coming to Him. Nobody wants to follow a person who lacks accurate knowledge of the one he follows.

> *"He also told them this parable: "Can a blind man lead a blind man? Will they not both fall into a pit? (Luke 6:39)*

Who wants to follow people who always have financial problems? That would be the question on the hearers' minds. Imagine Christ was not even bothered that there was a thief among the chosen twelve. He came with the good news and that thief was still going to have the opportunity to choose life until he refused it. That was his choice.

Notice that the Bible does not say, "For God so loved the church." We should learn a lesson from that. It means the people we speak against, God loves them. Do you want to be an effective person communicating Christ? Love is the key. We cannot be effective in winning people to Christ if we do not have a heart of love. If we bring them to Christ, it means we oppressed them by the words we spoke, and out of fear of hell they came. That kind of 'result' cannot be sustained. Only love sustains.

When we give love, we give freedom. Nobody can love without freedom. The love of God destroys the slavery of sin, and sets us free to reciprocate God's love and love for one another. You might probably have noticed that a lot of the people that are wrongly communicating the good news are people that have a lot of problems with love. They are "damaged evangelists" who roll laws on people, insisting that they have to behave in a certain way before they can belong to Christ. If people have to change their looks or change their clothes or wear some kind of uniforms with their head covered, then it means we are yet to grasp the full meaning of the good news.

The good news is that through their freedom and uniqueness, the Spirit of God will transform them. Look at how different Christ was from us, yet He identified with us in His humanity. He had never known sin, yet He ate with sinners, saved sinners, lived among them and was not disturbed. It is a shame that we that were born in sin and conceived in sin cannot stand one another. We have been bringing people to church but we have been oppressing them to follow us. If we tell people they are going to hell where the fire is unquenchable, we have just oppressed them. They will probably follow us but out of fear and they will pass on the message of hell to their children and everybody else, and as such, multiply the communication of bad news.

Life is influenced by the communication we give out because life is influenced by the words that we speak and live. If we fail to communicate rightly, we will not have the right people. Our churches are filled with very critical and judgmental people who are offshoots of our wrong communication. But God did not send His son to condemn the world but to save the world through Him. So, there is obviously no need for the message of condemnation that we hear so often.

The purpose of Christ is to save the world and that should be the focus of evangelism. We are to go and save the world through Christ, rather than remind them that they are living in sin! They already know that; they don't need us to remind them. We should instead give them the answer, which is Jesus Christ.

> *"Whoever believes in him is not condemned, but whoever does not believe stands condemned already because he has not believed in the name of God's one and only Son."* (John 3:18)

Why does the word condemnation feature here? Is it not for those who do not believe? And that is a matter of choice. However, God wants us to focus on the good news so that people will be drawn to Him. If this is properly communicated, people will choose Christ instead of condemnation.

Have you noticed that when you tell young people not to do something that is when they go out of their way to do that thing? Some of us exasperate our children by talking to them in like manner. Instead of communicating good news to them, we often tell them negative things. We call them names that communicate bad news. For example, calling your child "empty-headed" is communicating bad news. I tell my children they are very intelligent and that there is nothing they cannot do because Christ is with them and by the grace of God I see the result of my good communication today!

However, this cannot be done by human intelligence. It is the work of the Spirit. When we allow our human nature to come in, we err and communicate wrongly. If we would be honest with ourselves, it is easy for us to see where we all blow it and the controlling spirit that makes us blow it. We must not allow anger to control our communication. God's wisdom teaches us to be silent when we are angry.

> *"For man's anger does not bring about the righteous life that God desires." (James 1:20)*

Instead of communicating evil in anger, we should receive grace to be silent.

> *"For there is one God and one mediator between God and men, the man Christ Jesus, who gave himself as a ransom for all men – the testimony given in its proper time. And for this purpose I was appointed a herald and an apostle – I am telling the truth, I am not lying – and a teacher of the true faith to the Gentiles." (1 Timothy 2:5-7)*

The Scripture is telling us that the only distributor of life that God has chosen is Jesus Christ, the mediator between God and men. That places a responsibility on us to communicate Christ accurately to people. We should tell His story all the time to all the people. Even before they know Him, they must hear His story and how He fits into everyday living. We must de-emphasize our pastors and our church; it is bringing unhealthy competition and division.

> *"Jesus answered, "I am the way and the truth and the life. No one comes to the Father except through me"." (John 14:6)*

It is time we come back to the basics. We should come back to the way. Christ is the way, communicate Him. He is the answer. It is impossible for the name of the church's general overseer or pastor to heal any person or do any good. Goodness is a fruit of the Spirit of Christ for nobody is good except Christ.

> *"Who gave himself as a ransom for all men – the testimony given in its proper time." (1 Timothy 2:6)*

This Scripture is telling us that Jesus Christ has paid for all the things that are inadequate in us. We have been bought from inadequacy. So, if inadequacy is bringing condemnation, the answer is Christ. Once we come to know Christ, that sense of inadequacy is replaced with the abundant life in Christ.

> *"The thief comes only to steal and kill and destroy; I have come that they may have life, and*

*have it to the full."* (John 10:10)

Somebody who is caught in sin needs to know how not to sin again and enjoy the abundant life in Christ. Sin cannot condemn us anymore unless we agree and condemn ourselves.

> *"Therefore, there is now no condemnation for those who are in Christ Jesus."* (Romans 8:1)

If we all start presenting this truth, the church will enjoy good health and growth. It is impossible for the church to grow the right way if Christ is not properly presented. This is the essence of true church growth. Church growth is not when we gather a huge crowd who are not hearing the Word nor are they hearing Christ; rather they are only hearing the pastor. That is the reason they believe the pastor is the Messiah and will queue up for hours just to see him. The truth is we only need Christ; we do not need any man.

We must also be careful how we allow people who are not yet mature in Christ to be leading prayers and Bible Study. Christ will hold us accountable. Imagine someone who does not know you well playing the role of an ambassador for you. There is bound to be misrepresentation!

> *"So do not be ashamed to testify about our Lord, or ashamed of me his prisoner. But join with me in suffering for the gospel, by the power of God."* (2 Timothy 1:8)

Mark the word 'testimony'. The first principle in communicating Christ is love. The second is testimony. In my evangelistic outreaches, I strive to share the testimony of my salvation. For instance, when I encounter people who are into drugs, I tell them that there is something far more powerful than drugs. That immediately gets their attention. I then seize the moment to present Christ and my testimony of how I was a member of a confraternity, a dreaded cult group in the university campuses all over Nigeria. I remember a man who was present in one of such meetings, he used to smoke a sack of cannabis a week but after my preaching, he gave up that habit. He actually ran mad due to his addiction to cannabis, but he is very normal today and very solid in the Word too.

After his conversion, I had to teach him to stop projecting me. He was fond of always telling people how I brought him to Christ. He was almost worshipping me. Today, many of us are simply following men. Some of them even have us as bodyguard and watchmen because we have been made to believe that the way to get anointing is by following men, just as it was in the days of Elijah and Elisha. This is not so.

> *"For the grace of God that brings salvation has appeared to all men. It teaches us to say "No" to ungodliness and worldly passions, and to live self-controlled, upright and godly lives in this present age, while we wait for the blessed hope – the glorious appearing of our great God*

> *and Saviour, Jesus Christ, who gave himself for us to redeem us from all wickedness and to purify for himself a people that are his very own, eager to do what is good. These, then, are the things you should teach. Encourage and rebuke with all authority. Do not let anyone despise you." (Titus 2:11-15)*

And what is the grace of our Lord Jesus Christ? Do you know we make Him known if we communicate Him well? We give grace to people instead of condemnation. What is making this Scripture a question mark and a problem is that the disgrace that makes all men run from God has been made known.

At one point before I became born again, I did not think being born again was good because people that were presenting Christ to me were not attractive. I felt if I belonged to this group my life would not be anything to write home about. Paul talked about becoming all things to all men. But the Christians I encountered then were far from what Paul was talking about. You could identify them by their grim faces, judgmental attitude, and their sorry state.

For people to listen to us, we must be attractive both within and without, otherwise, they will look down on us. Out of the abundance of the heart, the mouth speaks (Matthew 12:34). If we speak words that make people look down on us, it is because we are not letting Christ reign in us. Christ never had any problem of attitude with any person; nor did He have any issue with anyone belittling Him, whether rich or poor. He knew He was the Author of life. When we also have His life and have it abundantly, we won't have such problems. How can a Christian have an identity crisis? If Christ had been presented well to me, I probably would not have joined the cult. I could not get answers to some of the burning questions in my heart because the idea that was being presented could not provide the answers.

This means that when we meet a wicked person our focal point should be that Christ has paid the price for the wickedness he is practising and so he does not have to continue in it. We do not need to tell the person that he is hell-bound; he probably already knows that. We should instead let the person know that he or she could change and go to Heaven because Christ has paid the price for all wickedness.

I won a woman to Christ by sharing my testimony with her. Prior to that, she had felt she could not be a Christian because she was smoking and drinking beer. But I laughed and told her of my former life of drinking and smoking a packet of Benson and Hedges a day. That got her attention and I was able to use my testimony as a dragnet to bring her to the Lord. Years later, she married a man who was a virgin. They were so different but Christ made them compatible! He bound them together with perfect unity.

Often times, the problem is that, instead of presenting the attractiveness of Jesus Christ, we present our opinions, our creeds, secular education, and every other thing but Jesus Christ. We have to learn our message of the gospel well and tell it well again and again; it is a matter of continuous learning and practice. The Scriptures of John 3, 1 Timothy 2, and Titus 2 are all talking about love, testimony, and grace, which are very important components of evangelism. Who is love and what does it mean? Whose testimony is love and what is your testimony? If we do not know whose testimony love is and what our testimony is, we will not be able to love and understand that the people we call unloved, God loves them and we can love them too. If we do not realize that God has placed all men under grace, we will disgrace them through bad communication.

CHAPTER FIVE

# GUIDELINES FOR EFFECTIVE EVANGELISM

The purpose of evangelism is to save the lost and disciple converts in the church.

> *"Then Jesus came to them and said, "All authority in heaven and on earth has been given to me. Therefore go and make disciples of all nations, baptizing them in the name of the Father and of the Son and of the Holy Spirit, and teaching them to obey everything I have commanded you. And surely I am with you always, to the very end of the age." (Matthew 28:18-20)*

The church is the Body of Christ where born again believers are nurtured and equipped with God's word so that they can function in holy relationships with God and man. It is important for the church to be healthy and germinal, rather than being unhealthy and terminal. When you are terminal you are not reproducing. For a church to be evangelical and be very effective in soul winning, it must have a germinal strategy, a strategy of reproducing. If Christ is not reproduced in our churches, what is reproduced is a lifestyle of the general overseer or pastor in charge. This is an error and it must be corrected. If your life is being duplicated exactly as it is by your son called Junior, it's an error because your son is supposed to be like Christ, not like you. We are meant to communicate the gospel.

> *"It was he who gave some to be apostles, some to be prophets, some to be evangelists, and some to be pastors and teachers, to prepare God's people for works of service, so that the body of Christ may be built up until we all reach unity in the faith and in the knowledge of the Son of God and become mature, attaining to the whole measure of the fullness of Christ. Then we will no longer be infants, tossed back and forth by the waves, and blown here and there by every wind of teaching and by the cunning and craftiness of men in their deceitful scheming. Instead, speaking the truth in love, we will in all things grow up into him who is the Head, that is, Christ. From him the whole body, joined and held together by every supporting ligament, grows and builds itself up in love, as each part does its work."* (Ephesians 4:11-16)

The church has not been called to organize programmes that will make the presence of Christ be felt, but to grow in Christ – as each member commits fully to a local church. The manifold wisdom of God is in the church (Ephesians 3:10)

The gospel is the message we have to communicate. Before I go into the basic fundamental of reaching the lost, it is important that we know that there is a difference between the gospel and the gospels. The gospel is the person of Jesus Christ. It is different from the gospels. The gospels are the presentation of the stories of Jesus Christ by Evangelists Matthew, Mark, Luke and John. These gospels are just perspectives of God's stories in Christ, presenting Christ as the life of God and the hope of mankind, telling every person to have their faith in Him.

The gospels are not a complete story of the gospel, hence we cannot depend on just the gospels. That is why we depend on the Spirit. Jesus did not say wait until the writing of the Bible before you begin to minister, He said, wait until you receive My Spirit before you go and minister. But the Spirit never veers off from the gospel.

Evangelist Matthew in writing his account of Christ was interested in presenting Him as the greatest personality - greater than Moses so that all the Jews would know that there is nobody that can compete with Christ. In order to effectively communicate this, he explained how Elijah and Moses handed over their lives to Christ at the Transfiguration. And that did something to the minds of the Jews because in that encounter, Elijah and Moses, who were icons to the Jewish community submitted themselves to the Authority and Lordship of Christ.

> *"After six days Jesus took with him Peter, James and John the brother of James, and led them up a high mountain by themselves. There he was transfigured before them. His face shone like the sun, and his clothes became as white as the light. Just then there appeared before them Moses and Elijah, talking with Jesus. Peter said to Jesus, "Lord it is good for us to be here. If you wish, I will put up three shelters – one for you, one for Moses and one for Elijah." While he was still speaking, a bright cloud enveloped them, and a voice from the cloud said, "This is my Son, whom I love, with him I am well pleased. Listen to him!" When the disciples heard this, they fell facedown to the ground, terrified."(Matthew 17:1-6)*

That statement, "Listen to Him" did a lot of damage to the theology of the Jews. Matthew, a Jew, wanted them to know that true doctrine centres on Christ.

Mark, on the other hand, presented Christ as the All Powerful. If you read Mark, you will not see so many parables. He was not interested in the talk and teachings of Christ; he was more interested in the power and miracles of Christ. Luke's focus was on presenting the human aspect of Christ as a good physician going about doing good.

Apostle John was a total departure. He was presenting Jesus as God.

> *"In the beginning was the Word, and the Word was with God, and the Word was God." (John 1:1)*

He went back to Genesis to validate the claim that Christ has always been God, but He is the Word that became flesh and dwelt among us. Thus, he emphasized the deity of Christ. When you read with this understanding, it will make you grow and help you in presenting Him well. When we were in theological school, we were advised to stay closer to the gospels than the letters or the Old Testament because everything in the Bible is about Christ from Genesis to Revelation. Not only that, in the entire Old Testament there were prophecies about His coming and He came as foretold in the New Testament. When He came, they beheld His Glory, He chose His people, and He sacrificed Himself for the sin of the world.

> *"Yet to all who received him, to those who believed in his name, he gave the right to become children of God." (John 1:12)*

As an assignment, I would encourage every person reading this book to read the four gospels and find out how Jesus Christ communicated God the Father to the people. It will expose how far off we are in communicating Christ to people right now. How did Christ communicate Himself and the Father to the fallen world of His time? How did He communicate to the apostles? We are meant to be communicating Christ in the same manner He did.

## GETTING STARTED

The right question in communicating Christ is not "What should I say?" or "What should I do?" You can't answer that until you answer the most important question: "Who is my audience?" The way I will communicate with a youth will be different from the way I will communicate with an older person because they do not have the same desires, wants and expectations. However, Christ is the answer for the two groups of people and everybody. It is almost impossible to communicate effectively when you group children, youths and adults together. There has to be a time of separation for the unique presentation of Christ to various groups. The fact is each group has differences to settle in Christ and Christ settles them if our communication is apt and if we understand that He deals differently with each group.

Christ also presented Himself differently to the crowd, the disciples, and the experts of the law, the Pharisees and Sadducees. Why did He not spare the religious leaders of His day? It is because they were not listeners! They were very rebellious! And the method of presenting Christ to the rebellious is different from the method of presenting Christ to the obedient.

Jesus presented Himself and God differently to people like Nicodemus and the Samaritan woman. Nicodemus was a rich man who knew nothing about the life of the Spirit and the future. So, when he came to Christ (Rabbi) thinking that they were contemporaries, Christ immediately shut him off and promptly told him:

> *"I tell you the truth, no one can see the kingdom of God unless he is born again." (John 3:3)*

Nicodemus was an aristocrat, but a spiritually dead man. Although a knowledgeable man, he failed to realize that intellectual prowess does not make any man right with God. It is the Spirit that makes us right with Him.

However, the good about him was he wanted a private time with Jesus.

Some people do not speak about Christ. That could only be because they do not know Him. We cannot be quiet when we know somebody. Knowledge is power. If we truly know Him, we will see that He is like fire in our bones and we just cannot shut our mouths. Even when we try to shut our mouths, the fire would keep burning; until we speak, we are not comforted.

One of the favourite stories in the gospels is the one about the woman caught in adultery. Look at how Christ settled that issue in the gospel of John 8. Consider how He dealt with the people who brought the adulteress. In every right presentation of Christ,

Christ is the hope of glory (Colossians 1:27) and He is the light of the world (John 8:12).

The world is in darkness without Christ. I want us to think about the presentation of Christ in the entire Scripture and then start practising how to communicate Christ to our friends, acquaintances and relatives. If Christ is indeed our hope, and we have made Him our hope, communicating that hope should be easy. However, if we have not made Him our hope, then we will have to be merely memorizing the Bible and telling people letters.

> *"He has made us competent as ministers of a new covenant – not of the letter but of the Spirit; for the letter kills, but the Spirit gives life." (2 Corinthians 3:6)*

## GUIDELINES FOR COMMUNICATING CHRIST ACCURATELY.

1. **Be Open:** When we are open, we will know how to present Christ. Otherwise, we will go off point, presenting what does not relate to the issue. Listen to people and listen to the Spirit in order to know what to say. Do you know that fear can prevent us from being open? Be relaxed and listen. We have to study the Word of God and pray so that we can communicate accurately. Also, we must ensure to present Christ to people who are also open; who will be receptive, otherwise we will be wasting our time. We also need to interact with people

and maintain relationships. Mix with people, be free, and talk with people at your workplace or social gatherings. Be bold to present Christ when the opportunity presents itself. We cannot afford to be people that others avoid whenever we show up because of the wrong attitude or outlook.

**2. Be a Listener:** We must be good listeners. This entails being sensitive. That way the Holy Spirit gives us answers for our prospects. Discerning our moods and that of other people is vital. We know that not all moments are good for our moods. Being able to help people out of bad moods aids accurate listening and communication.

**3. Be Available:** We can only speak to somebody that is available and shows interest in hearing us. When communicating Christ, we need to watch people's responses and concentration. Sometimes, vital information is lost when people are distracted or absent-minded. We should not be bothered by people who are not available or present. Jesus said Mary had chosen what is better, that is, making herself available to listen to Him. (Luke 10:38-42)

**4. Be Sincere:** One way to know someone who is sincere when Christ is communicated is the type of questions they ask, and statements they make. Sincere people ask transparent questions with the desire to understand Christ. Sometimes, insincere people give themselves away by asking no question and portraying an attitude of 'just leave me alone' or 'I already know what you are saying'. Follow-up needs to be done on sincere people alone.

**5. Be an Identifier:** An identifier is someone who shows a high level of gracious understanding and mixes with whoever is receptive to Christ. Just like Christ identified with sinners. It means to identify with people at their point of weakness, as Christ identified with our sins even though He was without sin. Look at Paul's account:

> *"Though I am free and belong to no man, I make myself a slave to everyone, to win as many as possible. To the Jews I became like a Jew, to win the Jews. To those under the law I became like one under the law (though I myself am not under the law), so as to win those under the law. To those not having the law I became like one not having the law (though I am not free from God's law but am under Christ's law), so as to win those not having the law. To the weak I became weak, to win the weak. I have become all things to all men so that by all possible means I might save some. I do all this for the sake of the gospel, that I may share in its blessings."* (1 Corinthians 9:19-23)

Accurate communication is easy when we are in love with God and people.

> *"You are the salt of the earth. But if the salt loses its saltiness, how can it be made salty again? It is no longer good for anything, except to be thrown out and trampled by men." (Matthew 5:13)*

> *"And if anyone causes one of these little ones who believe in me to sin, it would be better for him to be thrown into the sea with a large millstone tied around his neck." (Mark 9:42)*

These two scriptures are telling us that when we are communicating, we must do so taking cognizance of the role of salt in life. Salt is used for seasoning and preservation. Speak words that are seasoned with grace and will preserve people, not destroy them.

> *"Love must be sincere. Hate what is evil; cling to what is good. Be devoted to one another in brotherly love. Honor one another above yourselves. Never be lacking in zeal, but keep your spiritual fervor, serving the Lord. Be joyful in hope, patient in affliction, faithful in prayer. Share with God's people who are in need. Practice hospitality.*
>
> *Bless those who persecute you; bless and do not curse. Rejoice with those who rejoice; mourn with those who mourn. Live in harmony with one another. Do not be proud, but be willing to associate with people of low position. Do not be conceited.*
>
> *Do not repay anyone evil for evil. Be careful to do*

> *what is right in the eyes of everybody. If it is possible, as far as it depends on you, live at peace with everyone. Do not take revenge, my dear friends, but leave room for God's wrath, for it is written: "It is mine to avenge; I will repay," says the Lord. On the contrary:*
> *"If your enemy is hungry, feed him;*
> *if he is thirsty, give him something to drink.*
> *In doing this, you will heap burning coals on his head."*
> *Do not be overcome by evil, but overcome evil with good." (Romans 12:9-21)*

Love is a powerful communication tool that we have. Communication is an act of giving right information verbally or non-verbally. Accurate communication is easy when we are in love with God. So make sure you are in love, otherwise, you are playing religion and will inadvertently force the law and condemnation on people.

> *"Be wise in the way you act toward outsiders; make the most of every opportunity." (Colossians 4:5)*

Here is another helpful hint: Don't just see an outsider and lose your guard and talk or behave to him anyhow!

> *"Let your conversation be always full of grace, seasoned with salt, so that you may know how to answer everyone." (Colossians 4:6)*

The key point here is 'full of grace'. When communicating Christ, we should avoid bringing up disputable issues or being unnecessarily critical of people or churches. We should instead put people under grace and dwell on the answer Christ has provided for the problem of sin, as well as let them know how to enjoy freedom in Christ. When you season beef, it becomes very tasty. Likewise, let people taste of your life and experience quality.

> *"So that you may know how to answer everyone." (Colossians 4:6b)*

Christ is the answer to everyone. We tend to reveal how enlightened or ignorant we are through our communication—When we speak, we reveal who we know, and who we are. In order to communicate rightly, we must have the spirit of accuracy, which is the Holy Spirit. No man in a sinful state can be accurate. We can only be accurate when we are veterans in the Spirit and we have this covenant that we nurture with the understanding that the Spirit will teach and guide us into all truth.

## SIMPLE WAY TO LEAD A PERSON TO CHRIST

It is imperative for all disciples of Jesus Christ to know how to lead people to Him. Disciples are spiritual directors guiding people to Jesus Christ, the head of the body so that they are not led astray. There are three aspects to our salvation when we are born again. These are:

**Reconciliation:** Being reconnected to God through the death and resurrection of Jesus Christ by faith.

**Reorientation:** Renewal of the mind through submission to Jesus Christ who is the Word of God.

**Regeneration:** Ability to reproduce as a result of restoration.

## PERSONAL PREPARATION FOR WITNESSING

1. **Make sure that you love and study the Word of God.** You can begin with your testimony and then lead the person on to the Word.

2. **Be prayerful!** Pray for opportunities, boldness and the right word. Pray before approaching the person, silently during the conversation with the person and after an encounter with the person by committing their progress to the Lord.

3. **Establish friendship by creating interest in Jesus Christ.** Be sincere and genuine in your love. Be all things to all men. Practice hospitality, be patient, do not pressurize. Be consistent in your words, attitudes, actions, testimony etc. Be humble and admit mistakes.

4. **Assess the real need of the person.** Check the spiritual condition, background, and felt-need of the person such as family background, educational background, purpose in life and ambition.

5. **Explain man's basic problem, which is sin.** Give God's solution to the sin problem and allow the Holy Spirit work.

6. **Present the gospel.** Let the good news of Jesus Christ wipe out the bad news of the world. Eternal life, kingdom power, wholeness and freedom are some of the benefits of the gospel.

7. **Prepare for theological objections.** Examples:

- All religions are the same or Christianity is a western religion
- Jesus is not God
- The Bible is not consistent
- Do Christians worship three gods?
- What about those who have not heard of Jesus Christ?

8. **Prepare for personal objections.** Examples:

- If God loves me (us) why do I suffer?
- I am beyond correction (incorrigible)
- I shall decide later
- Some Christians are worse than non-Christians

9. **Lead the person to receive Jesus Christ.**

Explain the steps:

- Admit your need as a sinner
- Turn from sin
- Renounce the devil and his works
- Accept Jesus Christ as Lord and Saviour
- Accept the Holy Spirit into your life to help you.

10. **Teach how to grow in Christ.**

- Live by God's Word
- Talk to God in prayer
- Be in fellowship in the church
- Share Jesus Christ with others
- Learn to walk in the Spirit, etc.

## A WORD OF ADVICE

There is a tendency for many people to feel personally responsible for the salvation of their family, friends and co-workers. They somehow come under the crushing burden of guilt and develop a sense of failure if their loved ones fail to respond positively to the gospel message. Many of us would be surprised to realize that even Jesus did not carry that kind of burden for the lost. Hear Him:

> *"All that the Father gives me will come to me, and whoever comes to me I will never drive away."* (John 6:37)

> *"No one can come to me unless the Father who sent me draws him, and I will raise him up at the last day." (John 6:44)*
>
> *He went on to say, "This is why I told you that no one can come to me unless the Father has enabled him." (John 6:65)*

Clearly, Jesus knew that the responsibility for conversion ultimately rests with the Father and He submitted to the Father's authority and discretion in that regard. Notice that at the initial stage, the brothers of Jesus did not believe in Him as the Messiah.

> *"Jesus' brothers said to him, "You ought to leave here and go to Judea, so that your disciples may see the miracles you do. No one who wants to become a public figure acts in secret. Since you are doing these things, show yourself to the world." [5] For even his own brothers did not believe in him." (John 7:3-5)*

Do you notice the tone of scorn and mockery in the voice of the brothers of Jesus? If His brothers rejected Him, we should not be surprised or offended if our family members and friends reject, persecute or make fun of us. Does this mean that we should not do anything about our faith since it is God that draws men to Himself? Of course not! We should be ready at all times to testify of what the Lord has done for us and accurately proclaim God's plan of redemption for mankind.

We should talk about our faith, live it and invite others to taste of the goodness of the Lord! (Psalm 34:8)

It is important that we face the fact that sometimes our offer may be accepted outright; at other times, response to it might be delayed or perhaps not forthcoming at all. But that should not trouble or discourage us. The brothers of Jesus initially rejected Him in spite of His words and works. However, later on in life, James who was possibly the eldest of Jesus' brothers was converted and became the head of the Jerusalem church. He later wrote the New Testament letter, "The Epistle of James." Jude, the writer of the epistle with the same name is also believed to be the Lord's brother. The conclusion of the matter is that the person who hears the word is responsible for responding in faith while the person who shares the gospel is responsible for communicating faithfully and accurately.

## FOLLOWING UP A NEW CHRISTIAN

Following up a new convert into the body of Christ is the process of systematic help that is rendered to a new Christian so that he can grow towards maturity and fruitfulness. When we lead another person to the Lord, we have a responsibility of making sure that they are followed up in order for growth to take place. This can be done personally or by another person you can entrust with this responsibility. The goal is to present every person mature in Christ.

> *"We proclaim him, admonishing and teaching everyone with all wisdom, so that we may present everyone perfect in Christ." (Colossians 1:28)*

Remember that we are not called to make converts, because converts may change their minds. We are called to make disciples who are committed to Jesus Christ. In following up a new convert, it is advisable to have a disciple of same age group and gender as that of the new Christian to do this work. This helps to solve practical problems with empathy. The disciple's spiritual life, however, must be in order. The follow up must be done prayerfully and with flexibility, as led by the Holy Spirit. It is better to be a person-oriented disciple rather than a programme-oriented one. The key to this is to understand relationship principles in the church.

These are some of the follow-up tips that must be in place:

1. Give assurance of salvation. Encourage the new Christian to share why he made his commitment to Jesus Christ. Then, offer some textual teachings for assurance of salvation. E.g. Rom. 3:23; 6:23; Jn. 3:16 etc.

2. Emphasize the importance of studying the Bible daily. Have a devotional method of study (2 Tim. 2:15).

3. Teach the new believer how to pray and the importance of a lifestyle of prayer. Warn against possible hindrances to prayer.

4. It is pertinent that the new believer understands how to live according to God's will by putting Jesus Christ first at all times.

5. The new believer must not ignore walking in the Holy Spirit from the onset. The new convert must know the role of the Holy Spirit, the baptism of the Holy Spirit and the need for a continued walk in the Holy Spirit.

6. The new believer must be taught not to forsake the assembly of the saints- the church. Explain what is needed in the church and ways in which believers can share with others.

7. The new Christian must be encouraged to witness to others. Help the believer to prepare his personal testimony.

## CHAPTER SIX

# LIFESTYLE EVANGELISM

Earlier on, I made it clear that when we are communicating Christ, we are supposed to communicate His grace and His love. The Scripture is "for God so loved the world" (John 3:16), not 'for God so hates sin'. Yes, He hates sin, but He loves the world, and He wants to save the world. So when we are preaching, it is the grace of God in Christ we communicate. That is what makes Jesus Christ attractive to sinners, especially when they get to understand the forgiveness of God in Christ. We may think this approach is too liberal, tolerant and indulgent but that is the biblical standard.

In preaching Christ, it is inevitable that the gospel will attract all kinds of people. God will do the separation at the proper time.

> *"Jesus told them another parable: "The kingdom of heaven is like a man who sowed good seed in his field. But while everyone was sleeping, his enemy came and sowed weeds among the wheat,*

> *and went away. When the wheat sprouted and formed heads, then the weeds also appeared. "The owner's servants came to him and said, 'Sir, didn't you sow good seed in your field? Where then did the weeds come from?' "'An enemy did this,' he replied. "The servants asked him, 'Do you want us to go and pull them up?' "'No,' he answered, 'because while you are pulling the weeds, you may root up the wheat with them. Let both grow together until the harvest. At that time I will tell the harvesters: First collect the weeds and tie them in bundles to be burned; then gather the wheat and bring it into my barn.'" (Matthew 13:24-30)*

Have you sat down to think about Grace? Have you thought about the fact that God has riches in Christ, forgiving people their sins when they do not deserve it? Do you know that the heart of God is a heart of mercy and that His mercy exalts? That is what to present to people. It is a terrible thing to be an evangelist and your message is all about what God hates. There is no way a sinner will not want to listen if he understands that he has hope to be saved and escape hell.

In evangelism, it is important to communicate the message that will transform lives. We are to give the message that will make people receptive to the transformation that will take place when Christ is allowed.

## WHAT IS LIFESTYLE EVANGELISM?

Lifestyle evangelism is all about modelling Christ and His values in our thought, speech, actions and conduct. The theology of lifestyle evangelism originated from God's incarnation in Christ who came to dwell among mankind. For God to reach mankind, He had to become man and left His throne in heaven to live in a human setting through conception and birth. It is the coming down of God to become man in order to share humanity with us. The implication is, if we are going to be true communicators of Christ, let us be human and relate like Jesus. As a result, people can look at our lifestyle and see what makes us different from them.

Every one of us must be in a relationship, not just with believers, but also with unbelievers. If we have no relationship with unbelievers then we are not serious about evangelizing and winning them to Christ. The relationship should be defined and the Bible has defined it for us.

> *"Do not be yoked together with unbelievers. For what do righteousness and wickedness have in common? Or what fellowship can light have with darkness? What harmony is there between Christ and Belial? What does a believer have in common with an unbeliever? What agreement is there between the temple of God and idols? For we are the temple of the living God. As God has said: "I will live with them and walk among*

> *them, and I will be their God, and they will be my people."* (2 Corinthians 6:14-16)

We must not be equally yoked with unbelievers. However, if there is no relationship at all, we will be very ineffective in our witnessing. My professor in theological school once challenged us by saying "If you do not know that you need to be in a relationship with that Muslim mechanic of yours so that you could pray and begin to work on how to influence him for Christ, then you are not serious about communicating Christ. How many of you have smokers and drunkards visiting you? You have created fences! How then can you reach them? How can there be an outreach when there is a fence?"

The church is not growing because we have mistaken separation for isolation. It is very important for every Christian to know how to be in a relationship, just like Jesus did and communicated God to the people in His time. When we communicate with people we do not know; we are very vulnerable to error and assumptions. Those assumptions and error have also led to the misinterpretation of scriptures. I am not meant to be guiding people and putting pressure on them to obey God. I am meant to direct them to Christ and leave them to make their choice and Christ will be the judge of that, not me. We must be careful how we judge people by how they look, what they wear and other things we know nothing about or we should not concern ourselves with.

> *"Since the children have flesh and blood, he too*

*shared in their humanity so that by his death he might destroy him who holds the power of death – that is, the devil – and free those who all their lives were held in slavery by their fear of death. For surely it is not angels he helps, but Abraham's descendants. For this reason he had to be made like his brothers in every way, in order that he might become a merciful and faithful high priest in service to God, and that he might make atonement for the sins of the people. Because he himself suffered when he was tempted, he is able to help those who are being tempted." (Hebrews 2:14-18)*

From this scripture, we can see how Jesus has the authority of experience. In lifestyle evangelism, our lives are meant to influence people where we find ourselves whether at work or play, school or where we live. People should be able to see the difference in our lives and be drawn to Christ. If Jesus did not become man, He might not have had the authority to tell us that we should not fall into temptation. Somebody once had the audacity to say that God does not know what it means for a man not to marry; otherwise, there should be no question when a 52-year old unmarried man commits fornication. But Jesus went through life without fornicating! He was tempted in every way but did not sin.

*"For we do not have a high priest who is unable to sympathize with our weaknesses, but we have one who has been tempted in every way, just as*

> *we are – yet was without sin. Let us then approach the throne of grace with confidence, so that we may receive mercy and find grace to help us in our time of need."* (Hebrews 4:15-16)

In lifestyle evangelism, there are stages. First is the stage of meeting the person and introductions. This is followed by the stage of getting to know each other. You must not take off with 'Accept Christ and you will go to heaven; reject Him and you go to hell'. It is important to have a human setting from where we launch out. If you work in the corporate world for instance, you should be known as somebody attractive and pleasant, not as somebody who does not take nonsense or someone critical of the way people look or dress.

As an evangelist, how do you win people if you are not friendly? Is it by fire? By the time you threaten people with hell, they may give in without trusting in the message. This is called evangelism by fire. Converts from this method never get to know love because fear is the opposite of love, and there is never fear in love. You did not bring love, you brought fear and in order for them not to go to hell, they knelt down and repeated words after you.

> *"Because he himself suffered when he was tempted, he is able to help those who are being tempted."* (Hebrews 2:18)

Some of us act like we have never been tempted or never

sinned. That is the reason people do not believe us because they know that it is a lie. All human beings have strengths and weaknesses. We are accurate when we point only to Christ. Only the Spirit is accurate and He gives us proficiency in communicating Christ.

> *"The Spirit of the Lord is on me, because he has anointed me to preach good news to the poor. He has sent me to proclaim freedom for the prisoners and recovery of sight for the blind, to release the oppressed, to proclaim the year of the Lord's favor." Then he rolled up the scroll, gave it back to the attendant and sat down. The eyes of everyone in the synagogue were fastened on Him, and He began by saying to them, "Today this scripture is fulfilled in your hearing." (Luke 4:18-21)*

If the Spirit of the Lord is upon us, then it would be easy for the Lordship of Christ to be made manifest and we will not perpetuate error. The Spirit of the Lord is called the Spirit of Truth. Anytime you maintain truth, you cannot be inaccurate because truth and error are opposites. By our role, we are all meant to share Christ; thus, we are all preachers even though we may not have the gift of preaching .

> *"The Spirit of the Lord is on me, because he has anointed me to preach good news to the poor. He has sent me to proclaim freedom for the prisoners and recovery of sight for the blind, to release the*

> *oppressed." (Luke 4:18)*

Is it not true that the blind are the people we often overlook in our church membership drive? Instead, we focus on attracting the rich so that our tithes and offerings can increase. This attitude negates the spirit of missions; it is more like a project we are engaged in.

> *"On my account you will be brought before governors and kings as witnesses to them and to the Gentiles. But when they arrest you, do not worry about what to say or how to say it. At that time you will be given what to say, for it will not be you speaking, but the Spirit of your Father speaking through you." (Matthew 10:18-20)*

Jesus is imploring us in these scriptures to depend totally on the Holy Spirit because when communicating Christ, there will be persecution from people who hate this Christ that you are communicating. However, we are not to worry about how to respond to them because the Spirit of accuracy, the Holy Spirit, has been given to us. God is always speaking, but the problem is that we do not always listen and so we do not hear.

When relating to people and witnessing Christ, He says, "I will never leave you and I will never forsake you" especially when we operate under this great commission. To be effective communicators of this gospel in lifestyle evangelism, we must also demonstrate the life-changing power in the gospel by prayerfully healing people and casting out demons as Jesus did. Sometimes we bring invalids and make them more invalid in the church, Christ did not do that. We need to become people that are dependent totally on the Holy Spirit.

Do you know what you are communicating when you meet felt needs by helping somebody who is in need? Jesus did not just communicate by words; He healed the sick and fed five thousand people.

> *"how God anointed Jesus of Nazareth with the Holy Spirit and power, and how he went around doing good and healing all who were under the power of the devil, because God was with him." (Acts 10:38)*

Do you know what it means to stay in a home and pray for a dying child and the child comes alive? Do you know what that communicates? God, by His grace, gave me His anointing, the same Spirit to cast out demons of madness in a man who was addicted to cannabis and became insane. He became sound, got his children back from the government, and his wife discontinued the divorce proceedings against him and reunited with him. Today he is a deacon in his local church.

Instead of threatening people with hell, get involved in their lives lovingly. When we allow the Spirit of God to help us get involved in other people's lives and meet their needs, we would be surprised at the results that we would get.

> *"You are the light of the world. A city on a hill cannot be hidden. Neither do people light a lamp and put it under a bowl. Instead they put it on its stand, and it gives light to everyone in the house. In the same way, let your light shine before men, that they may see your good deeds and praise your Father in heaven." (Matthew 5:14-16)*

These scriptures are very important for evangelism. When people are in trouble and they come to us and their problems are solved, they are likely to stay put. Any right thinking person will not leave a solution ground for a problem ground. Be armed with love and grace. Give hope to the hopeless. Enlighten the blind, decorate the needy, and show future to the youth.

Let sinners understand that there is forgiveness for sin; do not say that they are doomed. Let the unfortunate know that there is no misfortune in Christ. As long as there is life, there is hope in Christ. That is how to spread the good news and make Christ attractive. He is able to handle every person's problem.

In lifestyle evangelism, let people see what you do and what you do not do. In the simplicity of your faith, let them come and ask, "Who are you really? I love your lifestyle, you are not harassed, I love the way you are always at peace even when times are difficult." That is how lifestyle evangelism works. Not people hearing you sing in church only to see you cry at home because you couldn't afford your house rent.

That kind of lifestyle makes Christ a debtor who owes people.

A scripture that will help us:

> *"Though I am free and belong to no man, I make myself a slave to everyone, to win as many as possible. To the Jews I became like a Jew, to win the Jews. To those under the law I became like one under the law (though I myself am not under the law), so as to win those under the law. To those not having the law I became like one not having the law (though I am not free from God's law but am under Christ's law), so as to win those not having the law. To the weak I became weak, to win the weak. I have become all things to all men so that by all possible means I might save some. I do all this for the sake of the gospel, that I may share in its blessings." (1 Corinthians 9:19-23)*

This is the heart of lifestyle evangelism. Our freedom should be to serve others, not the other way round. We become accurate in the Spirit when we become all things to all men. If we are not influencing people to know Christ, then we should examine ourselves whether we are truly in the faith.

> *"Examine yourselves to see whether you are in the faith; test yourselves. Do you not realize that Christ Jesus is in you – unless, of course, you fail the test?" (2 Corinthians 13:5)*

Test yourselves. Do you know yourself that Jesus Christ is in you? Unless indeed you are disqualified. This has nothing to do with going to Bible School to learn theology. Many have gone to theological schools just like those I went to school with, but they are not using it. God did not send the fishermen He called to theological schools.

> *"Devote yourselves to prayer, being watchful and thankful. And pray for us, too, that God may open a door for our message, so that we may proclaim the mystery of Christ, for which I am in chains. Pray that I may proclaim it clearly, as I should. Be wise in the way you act toward outsiders; make the most of every opportunity. Let your conversation be always full of grace, seasoned with salt, so that you may know how to answer everyone."* (Colossians 4:2-6)

That is an evangelistic thrust right there. I was very impressed when somebody shared a story about one of our deacons in church. He was driving to work with another church member when the car in front of him broke down. Even though he was in all white outfit, he alighted from his car and helped to push the car out of the road. That is evangelism. By that act, he helped to clear the road for other road users, as well as for himself. You cannot tell how much the man has been impacted. Their parts could cross in the future and he just might remember the gesture. His light had shone before the man.

There is a similar story in the Bible.

> *"In reply Jesus said: "A man was going down from Jerusalem to Jericho, when he fell into the hands of robbers. They stripped him of his clothes, beat him and went away, leaving him half dead. A priest happened to be going down the same road, and when he saw the man, he passed by on the other side. So too, a Levite, when he came to the place and saw him, passed by on the other side. But a Samaritan, as he traveled, came where the man was; and when he saw him, he took pity on him. He went to him and bandaged his wounds, pouring on oil and wine. Then he put the man on his own donkey, took him to an inn and took care of him. The next day he took out two silver coins and gave them to the innkeeper. 'Look after him,' he said, 'and when I return, I will reimburse you for any extra expense you may have.' "Which of these three do you think was a neighbor to the man who fell into the hands of robbers?" The expert in the law replied, "The one who had mercy on him." Jesus told him, "Go and do likewise."" (Luke 10:30-37)*

In this parable, Jesus indicted church folks who did not understand they had a responsibility to assist the wounded man. It was an unbeliever, a Samaritan, who came to his help, took him to the hospital, and paid his bills. Jesus now posed the question: Who is the real evangelist here (Paraphrased)? Notice the pride and prejudice in the Jews answer.

And he said, "He who showed mercy on him." Instead of him to say "the Samaritan", he instead chose to use the word "he". Why? The Jews hated the Samaritans so much that they could not bear to call them by name. Jesus ended that story by telling them to do likewise.

> *"Be wise in the way you act toward outsiders; make the most of every opportunity. Let your conversation be always full of grace, seasoned with salt, so that you may know how to answer everyone."* (Colossians 4:5-6)

## BROADVIEW EVANGELISM VS. LIFESTYLE EVANGELISM

This view of communicating Christ, called the Broadview evangelism, is not necessarily different from lifestyle evangelism; it is just broader, incorporating lifestyle evangelism into it. That is, after agreeing with lifestyle, it goes further, broader and wider in scope. The critical point of this view is that the gospel itself carries God's power and it is able to save anybody wherever and whenever it is communicated. In other words, wherever you are and whenever the Holy Spirit wants you to communicate Christ, there is inherent ability in the gospel to convict the listeners and win souls to Christ. This view seeks to prevent a situation where we limit ourselves and think that unless there is an on-going relationship we cannot succeed in soul winning. When we are led by the Spirit of Christ to communicate Him, there is power in what we say to bring about conviction and repentance.

> *"For the word of God is living and active. Sharper than any double-edged sword, it penetrates even to dividing soul and spirit, joints and marrow; it judges the thoughts and attitudes of the heart." (Hebrews 4:12)*

We must not come to the point where we feel we don't need to preach the gospel; that all we need to do is live out the truth of Christ for people to see and be persuaded. As important as lifestyle evangelism is, we must not fail to proclaim the gospel message through crusades, outreaches and one-on-one witnessing.

All believers are called to communicate the gospel while the Holy Spirit convicts the world of sin, righteousness and judgment. Let us look at some scriptures for references.

> *"We are therefore Christ's ambassadors, as though God were making his appeal through us. We implore you on Christ's behalf: Be reconciled to God. God made him who had no sin to be sin for us, so that in him we might become the righteousness of God." (2 Corinthians 5:20-21)*

> *"But I tell you the truth: it is for your good that I am going away. Unless I go away, the Counselor*

> *will not come to you; but if I go, I will send him to you. When he comes, he will convict the world of guilt in regard to sin and righteousness and judgment: in regard to sin, because men do not believe in me; in regard to righteousness, because I am going to the Father, where you can see me no longer; and in regard to judgment, because the prince of this world now stands condemned." (John 16:7-11)*

When we communicate Christ, we must put in view the following:

1. **The hope of heaven.** In other words, our hope is not just here on earth; every message of true evangelism must have heaven in it.

> *"And he said: "I tell you the truth, unless you change and become like little children, you will never enter the kingdom of heaven. Therefore, whoever humbles himself like this child is the greatest in the kingdom of heaven." (Matthew 18:3-4)*

2. **The reality of hell.** Since heaven is our hope, it shows the reality of hell as a real place. But that should not be the focus of the message; it should, however, get a mention.

> *"Then I saw a great white throne and him who was seated on it. Earth and sky fled from his presence, and there was no place for them. And I*

*saw the dead, great and small, standing before the throne, and books were opened. Another book was opened, which is the book of life. The dead were judged according to what they had done as recorded in the books. The sea gave up the dead that were in it, and death and Hades gave up the dead that were in them, and each person was judged according to what he had done. Then death and Hades were thrown into the lake of fire. The lake of fire is the second death. If anyone's name was not found written in the book of life, he was thrown into the lake of fire." (Revelation 20:11-15)*

3. **The brevity of life - life is too short.**

*"The length of our days may is seventy years – or eighty, if we have the strength; yet their span is but trouble and sorrow, for they quickly pass, and we fly away." (Psalm 90:10)*

**4. Decision.** Finally, the necessity of right decisions.

*"So, as the Holy Spirit says: "Today, if you hear his voice, do not harden your hearts as you did in the rebellion, during the time of testing in the desert." (Hebrews 3:7-8)*

CHAPTER SEVEN

# HOLY SPIRIT DISCERNMENT IN EVANGELISM

## CULTURE VS. THE GOSPEL

To communicate Christ accurately, we must learn to differentiate between the gospel and culture of a people. Generally speaking, culture describes the characteristics of a particular group of people, defined by their language, religion, food, architecture, social habits, arts and entertainment. There is often a tendency among Christians to confuse culture with the message of Christ. For instance, circumcision among the Jews is a cultural practice embedded in Judaism. In the New Testament, circumcision has been replaced with crucifixion.

The same goes for dressing. We must understand this so that we do not bring back a cultural trait and present it as the gospel - like the Judaizers that Paul preached against.

> *"A woman must not wear men's clothing, nor a man wear women's clothing, for the Lord your*

> *God detests anyone who does this." (Deuteronomy 22:5)*

Many people have taken this scripture to mean that women should not wear trousers while men should abstain from women's clothing. But this is a cultural thing. You cannot, for instance, preach against wearing of skirts by men in Scotland. That is their culture. In the same way, it is an error to preach as some do today that a woman should not wear trousers. The Bible verse above clearly refers to "garment"; it did not say trousers. And that statement was made from a cultural standpoint that warns against behaving like pagans.

In addition, history teaches us that wearing trousers is not a strictly masculine thing. We confuse people when our evangelism does not separate culture from the gospel. We must not forget that the gospel has universal application; there is no African gospel or American gospel. If the message cannot be applied to every context then it is not the true gospel.

Let me deal with another contentious issue here. Ephesians 5:18 says:

> *"Do not get drunk on wine, which leads to debauchery. Instead, be filled with the Spirit."*

Is this statement by Apostle Paul cultural or the gospel? It is gospel because it cuts across wherever you are and whatever you wear; skirts or trousers. However, it is not the gospel to condemn those who drink wine. It is a tradition. Be careful not to make a doctrine out of traditions that are disputable. It is okay if you decide not to drink as a mark of personal sanctification but then don't condemn people who drink and make it look like they are hell-bound. The same Paul tells Timothy to take a little wine for his health. This is because the boy needs a measure of alcohol for medicinal purposes. Drinking is different from being drunk, for drunkenness is ungodly.

> *"Stop drinking only water, and use a little wine because of your stomach and your frequent illnesses." (1 Timothy 5:23)*

The gospel message is not about food and drink.

> *"For the kingdom of God is not a matter of eating and drinking, but of righteousness, peace and joy in the Holy Spirit." (Romans 14:17)*

Of course, we need to teach people that they should be addicted to Jesus, and not to alcohol. People need to know that getting drunk robs them of peace and joy that is available in Christ. Some people drink as some form of aphrodisiac, to get high or escape their problems. Here is His invitation.

> *"Come to me, all you who are weary and burdened, and I will give you rest. Take my yoke upon you and learn from me, for I am gentle and humble in heart, and you will find rest for your souls. For my yoke is easy and my burden is light." (Matthew 11:28-30)*

Our message is connect with Him who is the Highest to be high. Do not get drunk is gospel but do not drink is a tradition. Do you know that overeating is a sin? It is the sin of gluttony, just as drunkenness is the sin of over drinking.

**Going Native:** There are some people who, in Broadview Evangelism, forsake their own culture and take the culture of the people they are sent to. This is called going 'Native' in cross-cultural missions. There are some people who have disregard for their tradition and culture and when they enter into a new culture that Christ has sent them, they overwhelmingly accept it and deny their background. These are said to have gone native as the case may be. Please discern that God did not send you to enter another culture and become another person. When I was in America, God told me that I am not an American, but a Nigerian living in America. He made me understand that I was not sent to America to be Americanized.

**Culture Shock:** When the Europeans entered African culture in the colonial era, some of them could not identify with us as Christ did. They built mission houses, brought generators to power light for them while the indigenes they came to reach out to, lived in darkness. Some mission still operates like that till today. That is the worst mission any person can do. If we cannot identify with the people we are trying to reach, then we should not bother. Jesus did not do that. When we cannot identify with the people we are trying to reach because of what we are used to in our culture, we can become so incapacitated to reach them. In fact, we may end up appearing like another group of oppressors.

It is a sad thing that even people in the same culture make the same mistake. We have cases of pastors who preach a doctrine of pastoral distance. They live in secluded houses and are inaccessible by members of their churches and communities. How can a pastor be effective when he deliberately sets a distance between him and the flock of Christ under his care?

Jesus shared humanity with us for the purpose of winning us. God did not use tracts to win souls, neither did He write things in the sky. Jesus Christ, the Son of God, lived among people, walked with His disciples, ate with them, and shared in their joy, travails, and triumphs. As a pastor, once you distance yourself from the flock, they can no longer trust your message because you live in a world different from theirs. They assume, rightly or wrongly, that you cannot know them or feel what they feel, we must be discerning enough not to fall into the same error.

**Motives:** We also need discernment to weigh the motives of people who attend church or claim to have received Christ. This is especially crucial in an age where people are making a career out of ministry. We must realize that some people are in the church with wrong or impure motives.

> *"When Simon saw that the Spirit was given at the laying on of the apostles' hands, he offered them money and said, "Give me also this ability so that everyone on whom I lay my hands may receive the Holy Spirit."*
> *Peter answered: "May your money perish with you, because you thought you could buy the gift of God with money! You have no part or share in this ministry, because your heart is not right before God. Repent of this wickedness and pray to the Lord. Perhaps he will forgive you for having such a thought in your heart. For I see that you are full of bitterness and captive to sin." (Acts 8:18-23).*

Sometimes people claim to be born again but they actually want a career rather than to communicate Christ and His grace. Their goal is fame and fortune. They are hoping to fill the position of your assistant when you get to need one, hopefully making money in the process. A man handed over his congregation to an assistant and returned to the USA. When he came back after five years, he discovered that the church was no longer into evangelism as was the custom. When he asked why, the assistant said the megaphone got spoilt. The question is, should the spoilt megaphone stop the ministry from evangelism?

Discernment is also needed at the time of crisis in a person's life. When supposed converts hit a financial, health or marital crisis, be watchful to see what their response will be. Will they submit to the leadership of Christ or will they run to a native doctor or some spiritualist looking for some quick fix? It is in times of crisis that you know what a man truly believes. That period also presents us with a golden opportunity to witness Christ properly in order to help them.

You should also discern people's attitude during rites of passages, at birth, death, or transition into age groups. When people conform to all those traditional rites in order to belong or be accepted, it reveals where their allegiance is. When witnessing to people through the Holy Spirit, pay attention to their proverbs or myths in order to communicate in such a way as to demolish strongholds. Africans have a lot of proverbs and myths that say a lot about who we are. In witnessing to such people, it is imperative that we destroy the foundation of their demonic belief system to put them in Christ. Watch out for signs, tattoos, looks, dressings, and pictures. All of these suggest what people believe.

## TO THE UNKNOWN GOD

*"The God who made the world and everything in it is the Lord of heaven and earth and does not live in temples built by hands. And he is not served by human hands, as if he needed anything, because he himself gives all men life and breath and everything else. From one man he made every nation of men, that they should*

> *inhabit the whole earth; and he determined the times set for them and the exact places where they should live. God did this so that men would seek him and perhaps reach out for him and find him, though he is not far from each one of us. 'For in him we live and move and have our being.' As some of your own poets have said, 'We are his offspring.'*
>
> *"Therefore since we are God's offspring, we should not think that the divine being is like gold or silver or stone – an image made by man's design and skill. In the past God overlooked such ignorance, but now he commands all people everywhere to repent. For he has set a day when he will judge the world with justice by the man he has appointed. He has given proof of this to all men by raising him from the dead."*
>
> *When they heard about the resurrection of the dead, some of them sneered, but others said, "We want to hear you again on this subject." At that, Paul left the Council. A few men became followers of Paul and believed. Among them was Dionysius, a member of the Areopagus, also a woman named Damaris, and a number of others." (Acts 17:24-34)*

When Paul entered Athens, he saw a plethora of gods that the people worshipped. When he was preaching Christ to them, he told them the God he was presenting is the One in whom "we live and move and have our being." He is not one of the gods as they were making

Him be.

Please do not be ignorant when communicating the gospel message. It does more harm than good to the teachings of Christ. We must depend upon our helper and teacher, the Holy Spirit to show us what we need to know so that we communicate effectively. Most of the early disciples – those we call apostles – were fishermen; so education is not the key thing here. Discernment by the Holy Spirit is the real thing.

My passionate desire is for all believers to break down the barriers to effective communication of Christ. We need to return to the simplicity of the gospel message.

> *"But I am afraid that just as Eve was deceived by the serpent's cunning, your minds may somehow be led astray from your sincere and pure devotion to Christ."* (2 Corinthians 11:3)

It is time we wholeheartedly make the Bible our book of evangelism instead of creed and doctrines of men. Let us be careful and proficient, and in our hearts, set apart Christ as Lord. It is time for the redeemed of the Lord to say so. The more of Christ you know the better your lifestyle and the better you allow others to be free to hear Christ and be like Him.

# GREAT DECISION

Dear friend, if you have not given your life to Christ you have to do so now with no further delay. Roman 10:9-10 provides:

> *"That if you confess with your mouth, "Jesus is Lord," and believe in your heart that God raised him from the dead, you will be saved. For it is with your heart that you believe and are justified, and it is with your mouth that you confess and are saved."*

Therefore pray this prayer to the Lord:

Lord Jesus Christ, I come unto You. You are my Saviour. Come into my heart, wash me with Your blood, write my name in your Lamb's book of life.

Give me power over the devil, demons, untimely death, diseases, sickness, sin and over every work of the devil. Thank you, Jesus, for saving me. Now I know that I am Your child and that I am born again. Amen!

After this prayer please seek a bible believing church where you will grow spiritually. You can also contact us through our information as appearing in this book. Stay blessed!

# ABOUT THE AUTHOR

**Peter Unoarumhi** is the founder and Head Pastor of Cornerstone Anointed Church of Christ, Surulere, Lagos. He is a dynamic teacher of the Word whose life's work is to equip a new generation of worshippers serving the only true God, Jesus Christ.

He obtained a B.A. Degree from the University of Ibadan in Philosophy and Religious Studies before he travelled to the United States of America where he obtained an M.Sc. Degree in Missions from the Abilene Christian University, Abilene, Texas.

Peter believes in the quality life that only Jesus can give and sees the opportunity to serve others as a gift of Grace. His Ministry has recorded astounding miracles as proof that he is sent by God.

He is married to his best friend, Becky and they are blessed with three Children, Manuela, Debra and Joshua (a set of twins).

## *CONTACT US*

We believe you have been blessed by this book.
For more information, please contact us at:

**CORNERSTONE ANOINTED CHURCH OF CHRIST**

56, Nuru Oniwo Street, Aguda,
Surulere, Lagos.
+234 802 944 0240, 903 745 4858
E-mail: cacc_car@yahoo.com
www.cacc.org.ng

www.ingramcontent.com/pod-product-compliance
Ingram Content Group UK Ltd.
Pitfield, Milton Keynes, MK11 3LW, UK
UKHW022006190726
13853UKWH00004B/1757

9 798408 516193